"In the Christian realm, the velopment, and true life char a treasure trove of leadership sonal life examples, and practi  The writer parallels the prin. ......pture references and concludes that great leaders only need look to the Bible for 'all things leadership.' In addition, he provides workplace and organizational best practices, advice for numerous situations, and offers self-evaluating questions. This is a must resource for every leader's library!"

—**Kip Miller**, President and CEO, Eastern Industrial Supplies

"Thank you for taking the time to write this book. You have done the community of leaders a real service. I have never read a book on leadership that is more grounded in spiritual truth than *The Goldmine*. It provides a clear map for the journey to more effective Christian leadership, whatever the venue. The book is encouraging, refreshing, and challenging - I left the reading with some practical ways that I can improve as a leader."

—**Marshall Franklin**, COO, Bob Jones University

"I appreciate Mike LaPierre's desire to encourage Christian leadership in the everyday situations of life. His book, *The Goldmine*, is useful for any Christian who desires to be a Christ-like example in the environment in which the Lord has placed him. I would encourage every leader to procure this useful tool, as I am sure that it will be as much of an encouragement to them as it was to me."

—**Matt Ohman**, Pastor, Faith Baptist Church (Palmer, MA)

"*The Goldmine* by Mike LaPierre addresses the great need for a credible witness for Jesus Christ in the workplace and then provides the Biblical instruction necessary to make that happen. Mike's understanding of scripture combined with his experience in the marketplace have produced a resource that every Christian who does business in this world ought to have at his or her disposal. If believing people embrace the truths and principles of this book, their 'lights' will shine brightly for Jesus Christ!"

—**Mike Jones**, Pastor, Cornerstone Baptist Church (Oakdale, CT)

"Christian leadership is a call for all believers to not only share their faith, but also have a positive impact in the marketplace. *The Goldmine* will equip and challenge you to have that impact on the job."

—**Mike Raley**, Pastor, Victory Baptist Church (Raleigh, NC)

"The workplace for the believer can be wrought with peril. Thankfully, the Word of God provides all that we need for life and godliness. As you read through *The Goldmine*, you will find practical principles based upon God's perfect instruction manual. Mike's experience with the workplace and his application of God's Word make this book an invaluable resource for every believer who wants to impact those within their God-given sphere of influence with the Gospel of Jesus Christ."

—**Jeffrey Bateman**, Senior Pastor, Cornerstone Baptist Church (Scarborough, ME)

"In *The Goldmine*, Michael turns our attention above the fray of human culture to point us to the higher standard of what authentic, Biblical leadership looks like. His intentional, practical, and convicting use of Scripture goes right to the heart of our motivations and helps to anchor a leader's actions deep within Biblical truth. This book satisfies the reader with much more than worldly statements about secular leadership, inspiring us rather to be Biblical leaders that truly transform the world around us for the sake of Christ's Kingdom."

—**Justin Murphy**, Entrepreneur, Professor, & CEO of Your Creative People

"Why another book on leadership? I already have a couple of shelves dedicated to that subject. In the *The Goldmine: Claiming the Workplace for Christ*, my friend Michael LaPierre addresses an oft-neglected aspect of leadership development. He connects the dots in an incredibly practical way to challenge Christians to be strategically deliberate as we face the work day and the workplace environment. He awakens us to the reality of the clash of worldviews that confronts us every day. He challenges us to claim the workplace as ambassadors and stewards of the gospel, for the glory of God. As I read and re-read this book, I felt like I was listening to a well-equipped leader, humbly challenging his employees (disciples) to be the salt and light that they are called to be. Mike and I have served together internationally, and I know what he gives us in this book is not just theoretical, but practical advice given from one who is well-qualified and passionate about sharing his experience as an athlete, a corporate executive, a family man, but most of all a Christian who loves God and wants to glorify Him in every area of life, even the workplace."

—**Jeff Davis**, EMU International

"*The Goldmine* is an excellent resource for believers who want to be godly leaders in their workplace. This book is firmly planted upon the Word of God and filled with practical insights in navigating the challenges of today's work environment. The attention given to the topic of communication through listening loudly and speaking carefully are particularly helpful in challenging us to fulfill our God-given role to let our lights shine in our places of work."

—**Nate Petersen,** Senior Pastor, Adirondack Baptist Church
(Gloversville, NY)

The GOLDMINE

CLAIMING *the* WORKPLACE *for* CHRIST

MICHAEL J. LAPIERRE

HIGH BRIDGE BOOKS

HOUSTON

About the Author

Michael James LaPierre is a Brown University graduate with Bachelor of Arts degrees in both Organizational Behavior and Management and Political Science. He holds a Master of Business Administration degree from Clemson University with a focus on Entrepreneurship and Innovation. He is an author, motivational speaker, guest lecturer, and founder and current President of Christian Leadership Worldview International, LLC (clwi.org).

A former professional baseball player, his executive experiences over the past 30 years include VP of Sales, Director of Sales & Marketing, global strategist, entrepreneur, church servant/deacon, and community leader. His diverse executive background and nonprofit experiences have allowed him to gain a comprehensive understanding of the principles of leadership development. Those broad experiences include leadership positions on management teams in companies such as UPS, Arnold Industries, Lily Transportation, and Roadway Express.

With nonprofit, for-profit, ministerial, and athletic experiences as a backdrop, Michael has the proven ability to capture the essence and fundamentals of leadership training and development. He then relates those varied experiences in a communication style that is motivational, powerful, and relevant to today's employees, students, and organizational leaders.

Mike and his wife, Calie, have been married for more than 32 years. They have three adult children: Ryan, Kyle, and Lauren. They also have been blessed with four grandchildren: Emma, Julia, Cooper, and Tanner. Mike and Calie reside in Pickens, South Carolina.

To contact Mike about the possibility of speaking at your next leadership event and/or conducting a leadership conference/seminar, you can reach him via the following:

mikelapi@gmail.com
mike@clwi.org
www.clwi.org

Be ye doers of the word and not hearers only deceiving your own selves.

– JAMES 1:22

For by him all things were created, that are in heaven, and that are in earth, visible and invisible, whether they be thrones, or dominions, or principalities, or powers: all things were created by him, and for him: And he is before all things, and by him all things consist.

– COLOSSIANS 1:16-17

For God so loved the world, that he gave his only begotten Son, that whosoever believeth in him should not perish, but have everlasting life.

– JOHN 3:16

This book is dedicated to my wife, children, and grandchildren.

Mom, I love you, too!

CONTENTS

INTRODUCTION

I must confess at the outset of writing my second book on Christian leadership that this exercise has been one of the most productive spiritual times of my life. God has given to me the excitement, passion, and drive to explore a subject that is greatly needed in our times. I have been richly blessed and have been given back exponentially more than the time and energy required to write this book. The creation of this book has been a three-year-long process comprised of thousands of hours of research, Bible study, prayer, mediation, and thoughtful conversation with fellow believers. I am praying that, when Christians read this book, they will become better informed about our duty to impact the workplace (marketplace) and take decisive action to make a difference.

However, beyond the spiritual blessings of writing this book, I must also point out that this three-year timeframe in my life has been filled with intense spiritual warfare. The enemy is not pleased when we set out to proclaim the holy and righteous nature of our Savior. Satan is trying to lay claim and hold onto a spiritual realm and cultural manifestation (workplace) that is decidedly becoming more anti-God. It is no secret that a secular humanist mindset is being forced on Christians as the organizations we work in continue to create cultures that are incongruent and disparate to sound Bible doctrine and teaching.

Furthermore, a case can be made and argued that, without a proper understanding of our workplace responsibilities as Christians (Monday through Friday), our time with the Lord on Sundays will be much less meaningful. I am suggesting that the Lord's Day is the most important day of the week and, without proper preparation leading up to that special day, we would experience much less of His working in our lives. We shouldn't come to church on Sunday demoralized by the workplace environment from the preceding week or have a knot in the pit of our stomachs for what we are about to experience in the upcoming week. I believe that healthy churches have members who are adequately prepared for the workweek and come to church on Sundays invigorated by what the Lord will do through them the following week. Charles H. Spurgeon said,

> We begin our day with prayer, and we hear the voice of holy song full often in our houses. But many good people have scarcely risen from their knees in the morning before they are saluted with blasphemy. They go out to work, and all day long they are vexed with filthy conversation like righteous Lot in Sodom.[1]

Through this book, I want to offer an ideal, optimistic, and Christian perspective of the workplace that starts with a *Christian leadership worldview*. We are going to explore Christian leadership from three different perspectives. These three perspectives will serve as the underpinnings and foundation of what we are trying to communicate.

First, we will start with *relational* leadership. This element of leadership looks at the way we care about and interact with those around us. Relational leadership speaks directly to the *heart* of mankind. We serve a Savior who was the master at building relationships. We also serve a Savior who is greatly concerned with the heart condition of man.

Second, *conceptual* leadership relates to the way we think in the workplace environment. This aspect of leadership impacts the *mind* of mankind. Christ was concerned with the way we train, cleanse, and stimulate our minds with thoughts that are righteous and pure.

Third, we are going to explore *vocational* leadership and the way we labor when we are at work. The Bible has much to say about our diligence when engaged in workplace activities. These three forms of leadership engagement should all be fueled with our Christian testimonies and salvation experience, which should ultimately impact the *soul* component of leadership awareness and understanding. Yes, we are trying to create a dynamic workplace environment for the Lord!

Soul = Salvation and Christian Testimonies

Relational Leadership = Care = *Heart*

Conceptual Leadership = Think = *Mind*

Vocational Leadership = Labor = *Workplace*

Dynamic Environment for the Lord!

The second consideration and motivation for writing this book stems from the need for alignment. Christians currently operate in three primary realms that consume most of their time and energy. The church, family, and workplace realms are vital spiritual domains that must be conquered for the Lord. Unfortunately, the current relationship between each of these domains is nothing more than an intersection at best. In other words, the way that we exude and put on our Christian testimonies falls far short of complete and total alignment. The ways we relate, think, labor, and live out our Christian testimonies is different in each of those primary spiritual realms.

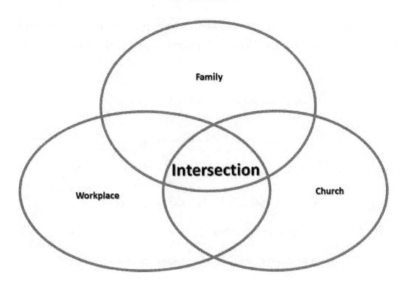

Some would argue that we are duplicitous in our efforts to put on the mind of Christ and speak with many tongues. How can we impact the world for Jesus Christ when we are speaking out of three sides of our mouths? When we are at work, we are one type of Christian. When we are with our family members, we are another type. And lastly, we put on that ceremonial church grin and smile when interacting with fellow believers while in the "house of the Lord."

Now, I must admit that I am giving you the fire-hydrant version of what is happening out there in the workplace by giving you a broadbrush. However, I believe that working Christians everywhere can relate to what I am saying. What we need is total alignment that begins with proper focus and prioritization.

Alignment

The final motivation for writing this book is what I will describe as the "call to action." I read something several years ago that stirred my spiritual sensitivities about the workplace. Notwithstanding, I had just concluded a 33-year stint in the corporate world and had experienced much of what I am writing about. Everything I experienced in the workplace is fresh, raw, and relatable.

In their book, *Integrity at Work*, Norman Geisler and Randy Douglass made several claims about the workplace that got my attention.

> One hundred twenty-two of Jesus's 132 public appearances were in the workplace.

> Forty-five of Jesus's fifty-two recorded parables had a workplace context.

> The church was founded by many business people.[2]

As I began to contemplate the depth and impact of those statements, I had one of those moments where the "lights went on." I thought, *If Jesus thought the workplace (marketplace) is so important as to spend a majority of His time there, then that is where I need to focus my time and attention for His glory.*

---

[1] *The Essential Works of Charles Spurgeon: Selected Books Sermons and Other Writings,* Edited by Daniel Partner (Barbour Publishing, Inc., 2009).

[2] L. Geisler and Randy Douglas, *Integrity at Work: Finding Your Ethical Compass in a Post-Enron World* (Grand Rapids: Baker Books, 2007).

Part 1

UNDERSTANDING THE PLAYING FIELD

1

Using Radars of Discernment

*Marketplace leaders must lay the spiritual foundation, strengthen the core, and then build the necessary muscle for a dynamic **Christian leadership worldview** and marketplace impact.*

The most difficult struggle for Christians in the workplace is having or maintaining the determination and planning ability on a daily basis not to let the flesh control our thoughts, motivations, and actions. We should be willing to let the Spirit of God permeate each facet of the workplace experience.

I know what you are thinking... *Much easier said than done!* Our success will hinge on the preparation, care, and discipline that we take prior to showing up to work. Have we adequately bathed ourselves in the instruction and precepts of God's Word? What part does prayer and meditation play in the workday? Do we have a God consciousness throughout the day, or are we so consumed with the details of "the work" that there is very little room for the Holy Spirit to influence and direct? Do we have a systematic and strategic way of finding the Lord each day at work before it's time to head home?

Average Christians everywhere have good intentions when they show up to work in the morning. Many set out with enthusiastic energy and want to exhibit the fruit of the Spirit so that others may see Christ in them. They hope to influence others in the workplace to draw them to a saving knowledge of Jesus Christ. But then, reality sets in. The stress, busyness, details, noise, and overall demands of our work environments quickly take us away to a singular focus on "the work" with little room for spiritual awareness and impact. We have probably all experienced this letdown at one time or another.

A general once said, "All strategy does not survive first contact with the enemy." Think about that statement for a moment. Even those who have a rock-solid plan in the first place will have to make numerous adjustments to their original plans. Things will happen, decisions will be made, and actions will be taken that we didn't anticipate. How much worse will it be for workplace Christians who don't have a spiritual plan of attack? Without a plan of devotion to the Lord, it will be almost impossible for well-intentioned, Bible-believing Christians to win the spiritual battle being waged in the workplace.

The spiritual battle is won by being separate and distinct unto the Lord and by not conforming to the standards of the world. The enemy wants to claim the workplace domain as his own, and we must allow our "radars of discernment" to provide the spiritual guidance that we need.

I sincerely believe that the taxing spiritual demands of the workplace will quickly exhaust our energies and diminish our resolve long before the mental or physical demands ever will. The oppression and aggregate exposure to anti-God realities take an immense toll on our Christian outlook and disposition. Therefore, we must ask ourselves, "How are we going to spiritually bulk up and stand tall in the midst of workplace challenges?" Because our success at work is primarily related to our spiritual cognition and fluency, marketplace leaders should lay the spiritual foundation, strengthen the core, and then build the necessary muscle for a dynamic *Christian leadership worldview* and marketplace impact. This begins with a healthy dose of reality and a spiritual recognition of the enemy.

The Spiritual Battle

> *For we wrestle not against flesh and blood, but against princi-*
> *palities, against powers, against the rulers of the darkness of*
> *this world, against spiritual wickedness in high places.*
>
> —EPHESIANS 6:12

If you have any doubt about the spiritual battle going on at work, take the time to compare the number of believers versus the number of non-believers you are interacting with on a daily basis. Then, reflect on the elements of the nonbelievers' belief systems and the corresponding worldviews. Some Christians will even try to argue that there are many good and moral people in the workplace who are kind, generous, and gentle. Unfortunately, many of our coworkers share beliefs that are in direct contrast to biblical and foundational instruction.

There should always be a large chasm between Christians and our nonbelieving counterparts in the workplace. If Christians are sincerely putting on the mind of Christ, this chasm should exist in numerous manifestations. This chasm will create a friction, negative energy, and intensity like you have never before experienced in your lifetime. After spending 33 years in the corporate world, I can unequivocally tell you that the contrast and division is both significant and evident as you conduct your business affairs during the course of the workweek. If you are a Bible-believing Christian who is devoted to his or her faith, a week will not pass without the evidences of the spiritual warfare rearing its ugly head. We are fighting a battle to have the spiritual, moral, and ethical courage to do what is right in a marketplace environment (customer environment) that can be aggressive, pressure-filled, and at times, extremely demanding. The enemy is currently thriving in the workplace!

For now, suffice it to say that the secular humanist's entire focus revolves around the greatness of mankind and his power to improve the conditions of this present world. I have dedicated an entire chapter later in this book to exploring the doctrines of this thriving religion.

THE ENVIRONMENT

And we know that we are of God, and the whole world lieth in wickedness.

—1 JOHN 5:19

To get a sense of the battles that are being waged in the world today, all one must do is to reflect on the things that we read in the local newspapers relating to the corporate, entrepreneurial, government, farming, nonprofit, teaching, and even religious circles across the globe. Do you recognize any of the following (sins) that apply to your specific workplace domain?

- Theft
- Discrimination
- Financial mismanagement
- Fraud
- Inappropriate comments
- Sexual harassment
- Data manipulation
- Lying
- Cheating
- Negligence
- Poor recommendations
- Marketing misrepresentation
- Revealing trade secrets
- Confidential information
- Trademark infringement
- Bribery
- Anti-trust violations
- Infidelity
- Contract non-compliance
- Lack of transparency
- Little white lie
- Small exaggeration

Although things may seem to be crumbling around us, we know with absolute certainty that, as Christians, we must lead. We must lead because we have the hope of eternity and a brighter tomorrow. We also know with absolute certainty that the antidote to the world's leadership ills all rests in the authority of the Word of God. I believe that the application of Biblical principles in today's business world has never been more important. When we rest in the power of His Word in the workplace, we will be transported from the mire, muck, and entanglements of organizational life to untold blessings from above and to new spiritual heights.

As we begin to understand the workplace playing field and use our radars of discernment, we must approach this mission field with joy and excitement. We should optimistically "consider it well" before engaging in our respective workplace endeavors (Prov. 24:32). While the battle is certainly daunting, in no way should we hang our heads in defeat. We should refrain from what I will call an "Eeyorean Complex" approach to work. If you recall, Eeyore is an A.A. Milne character from the *Winnie the Pooh* stories who seems to have a dark shadow following him everywhere he goes. Having a negative, pessimistic, defeatist attitude will surely play right into the enemy's hands. Satan always benefits when our workplace testimonies are less than Christ-like.

In no way is the intent of this chapter to promote fear and despair when mapping out the spiritual warfare in which we are engaged at work. On the contrary, I hope and pray that this chapter has helped to elevate our thinking, promoted additional awareness, and renewed our determination on the subject by acknowledging the many realities that we are faced with each day. It's an intense spiritual battle, one in which we need to be ready to engage at work. March on, Christian soldier. March on!

CHRISTIAN LEADERSHIP WORLDVIEW: PRINCIPLE #1

Christians should be determined to come to work with a well-thought-out plan for workplace devotion unto the Lord. Bringing a systematic and organized approach to combating the enemy will bring additional spiritual awareness for those who want to impact their workplace's culture for Christ! Allow the Holy Spirit to heighten your radars of discernment.

2

Navigating Moments of Truth

A moment of choice is a moment of truth.

—Stephen Covey

To say that Christians will experience moments of truth in the workplace is likely one of the most understated facts in this book. Bible-believing Christians everywhere will be bombarded with situations, decisions, events, personalities, and a host of other challenging workplace issues that will make one's hair stand on end. If you think that the organization you work for isn't susceptible or prone to these difficulties and may have reached a higher level of human maturity, please think again.

There isn't anything that the enemy enjoys more than to employ a divide-and-conquer strategy in the workplace, especially with and among Christians. Satan wants to create a toxic and divisive workplace environment where he can keep everyone on edge and at odds with one another. He wants an environment where egos dominate, self-centeredness ensues, pettiness thrives, intellectualism echoes, bickering festers, and the focus on upward mobility is front and center. Yes, he wants a cultural framework at work where it is all about "me and my needs." And while the corporate code of conduct and the employee handbook detail many of the moral and ethical standards of expected compliance, combatting some of the baser instincts of fallen man, they do little to address the numerous moments of truth that Christians will experience.

This book was written for the workplace Christians who won't rationalize, justify, and simply explain away their actions when faced with the standards of this world. They are Christians who will look deep into their souls and make decisions that line up with God's Word. This book is not for Christians who will knowingly and willingly let something slip by, pose an argument that suggests they are obligated to live by the rules of their employer, or even cast a blind eye to blatant outright breaches of the law. In this book, the challenge is to the person who has a *Christian leadership worldview* and will stand up and shout the alarm of wrongdoing when the precepts of God's Word are violated. Those are the Christian employees who are fully engaged and shrouded in the Spirit of God for the betterment of their organizations.

OUR RESPONSE

The Word of God gives us clear direction for how we are to engage and live out our faith:

> And be not conformed to this world: but be ye transformed
> by the renewing of your mind, that ye may prove what is
> that good, and acceptable, and perfect, will of God. (Rom.
> 12:2)

I absolutely love this verse! Is there any better instruction found for interacting with the world (of which, the workplace is part) than this? At a fundamental level, this verse is telling us, "Don't do this. Do this. And here's why…" So how do we apply Romans 12:2 when we are experiencing the unending onslaught of workplace dilemmas that come up each day? Let's contemplate our responses to a few of the potential workplace encounters:

- How should I respond to that sarcastic comment?
- How should I respond to a poor performance review?

- How can I lead in environments that are dominated by secular humanists?
- How can I get people to follow me?
- Am I exhibiting conversational intelligence?
- How should I act in pressure-filled situations?
- Should I laugh at an improper joke? How should I respond?
- What is my attitude like at work?
- Should I read and study my Bible at work?
- Should I pray through the work day?
- Should I witness at work?
- Are there things I can do at work to be a better leader?
- Am I communicating in the right way? How can I improve?
- Am I stealing time at work?
- Am I exercising my spiritual gifts and natural talents in the workplace to their fullest extent?
- What is my motivation to be at work?
- Am I reflecting the nature of a holy and righteous God?

We respond to the questions above by being obedient, applying key Biblical learning and the truth of God's Word, and renewing our minds with the precious tools the Lord has provided for us (e.g. prayer, meditation, Bible reading, fellowship, and worship). When we do this, the tasks and decisions at work, along with the associated spiritual warfare, will become much easier to navigate. While there will still be great challenges ahead, the renewing of our minds will also help to reduce the associated tension and stress. It will provide for the Christian leader an uncommon focal point and advantage that only he or she can envision and utilize by the leading of the Holy Spirit.

We have just scratched the surface of the thousands of potential workplace situations that will cross our desks. Fortunately, the solutions to these potential problems (opportunities) become much clearer when we are using the filter of God's Word to guide and direct. In addition to Romans 12:2 above, there are many other verses that point to our Christian responsibilities while at work. While the few verses listed below may not explicitly cite the workplace as the primary context, each has universal application for our Christian responsibility and duty.

> I beseech you therefore, brethren, by the mercies of God, that ye present your bodies a living sacrifice, holy, acceptable unto God, which is your reasonable service. (Rom. 12:1)

> Ye are the salt of the earth: but if the salt have lost his savour, wherewith shall it be salted? It is thenceforth good for nothing, but to be cast out, and to be trodden under foot of men. (Matt. 5:13)

> Ye are the light of the world. A city that is set on an hill cannot be hid. (Matt. 5:14)

As we navigate our moments of truth in the workplace, there is one final area of discernment and warning that we should address. Please, *do not let the small sins go unchecked.* Use wisdom and discernment in all decision-making, and stay away from the "gray" areas. There are many folks out there who enjoy operating on the edge. They begin to compromise on the small things, and before they know it, an avalanche is coming directly at them. This can happen to Christians just as easily as it can happen to nonbelievers. Let's use CEO Jeff Skillings of the former Enron Corporation as a case study.[1]

Enron – Jeffrey Skilling CEO

- West Aurora High School
- Southern Methodist University
- Harvard Business School
- Enron CEO
- Prison

Do you think it was Jeff Skilling's lifelong dream to "cook the books" and go to federal prison? Do you think he was scheming back in high school about how to deceive shareholders? No, more than likely, the intensity of the sin started with the little white lie and small exaggeration. He probably got very comfortable operating in the gray when the pressures and expectations of workplace performance started hammering him. Based on the beginning of his resume, one might think he would be running for office rather than going to jail! While Jeff Skilling may be the poster child for everything ugly and perverse about the corporate world and organizational misbehavior, he has had plenty of company over the years. Let's take a look at a few of the other scandals that have "shocked" the workplace.[2]

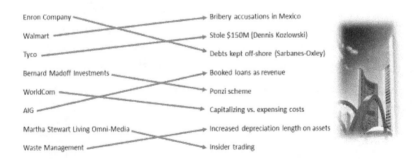

Enron Company	Bribery accusations in Mexico
Walmart	Stole $150M (Dennis Kozlowski)
Tyco	Debts kept off-shore (Sarbanes-Oxley)
Bernard Madoff Investments	Booked loans as revenue
WorldCom	Ponzi scheme
AIG	Capitalizing vs. expensing costs
Martha Stewart Living Omni-Media	Increased depreciation length on assets
Waste Management	Insider trading

Suffice it to say, when human beings operate outside of God's moral law in the workplace, bad things are bound to happen. There is no doubt that most of what God hates in Proverbs 6 can be seen in the legal proceedings above.

> These six things doth the LORD hate: yea, seven are an abomination unto him: A proud look, a lying tongue, and hands that shed innocent blood, An heart that deviseth wicked imaginations, feet that be swift in running to mischief, A false witness that speaketh lies, and he that soweth discord among brethren. (Prov. 6:16-19)

CHRISTIAN LEADERSHIP WORLDVIEW: PRINCIPLE #2

Christians should have an acute understanding of the complexities and entrapments of organizational life. Because of the untold pressures of the workplace, Christians must quell the old man within by the renewing of their minds. Praise the Lord He has given to us the unchanging roadmap of His Word for workplace decision-making, spiritual discernment, and warning.

---

[1] https://en.wikipedia.org/wiki/Jeffrey_Skilling

[2] www.accounting-degree.org/scandals/

3

THE LENS OF RESPONSIBILITY

*You cannot escape the responsibility of tomorrow by evading it
today.*

—ABRAHAM LINCOLN

What an awesome responsibility we have to leave an imprint on our places of work and their associated workplace cultures. With so many of our waking hours here on Earth dedicated to work, we must be diligent in making the best use of that time for the glory of God. We have one shot at this thing called a career. For many of us, our careers will span a timeframe of 30-40 years, at best.

It is the opinion of this author that we need to be activists in our approach for embedding our Christian values in the marketplace by leaving our markers everywhere we can. I also believe that the "Great Commission" is the starting point and our first job in order of priority.

> Go ye therefore, and teach all nations, baptizing them in the name of the Father, and of the Son, and of the Holy Ghost: Teaching them to observe all things whatsoever I have commanded you: and, lo, I am with you alway, even unto the end of the world. Amen. (Matt. 28:19-20)

When I think about the sacred responsibility of teaching, preaching, discipling, and demonstrating obedience unto the Lord at work in the 21st century, my mind is immediately distracted with the rules and regulations of organizational life that restrict us from performing our duties. Many companies will not allow us to verbalize our faith or even talk about religious things, let alone share the gospel message of Jesus Christ. On the other hand, we are asked to enforce corporate guidelines and policies while showing tolerance of stances that are clearly opposed to Biblical principles and doctrine. There are even those who believe that the doctrines of Christianity promote hatred and vitriol and should be considered to be on the level of hate crimes. How can we overcome these difficult challenges?

It must be stated at the outset that, when we are on company time and are expected to be working, we either must defer to the company's requirements or be guilty of stealing company time. However, each workplace environment will be different, and Christians will need to use a tremendous amount of wisdom and discernment when moving forward through these myriad issues. We will have to gauge the individual company's receptivity, then plan and act accordingly. Of course, there will be degrees of Christian tolerance, depending on the organization in which you work. Some have a zero-tolerance rule for religious engagement and activity while others encourage discussion at appropriate times (e.g. breaks, lunch time, etc.). We can overcome these challenges with a *Christian leadership worldview* that compartmentalizes each of our responsibility areas in a way that can't be called out and manipulated.

With much prayer and faith, you will begin to see your workplace environment (along with the organizational construct itself) in a spiritual realm and through a lens that will change your perspective on how you view work. There are three things to consider.

The Why

In *Start With Why*, Simon Sinek takes us on a journey to find out how great organizations achieve success. He writes,

> Great companies don't hire skilled people and motivate them, they hire already motivated people and inspire them.[1]

Sinek goes on to discuss the impact of fully understanding and then communicating *why* we do what we do instead of simply telling people about *how* we do something or *what* we do. In other words, the how and what is like show and tell. It's like dumping your briefcase on your customer's desk and telling them how and what your company does. This is the same approach every other organization uses with its customer base. By using this approach, you become another commodity just like everyone else. On the other hand, as Sinek teaches, "If you follow your why, then others will follow you."[2] The *why* should inspire and motivate us and others to new levels of achievement and leadership.

When thinking about our Christian lens of responsibility in the workplace, we can take a page out of Simon Sinek's playbook and start with a *why* premise. While the book, *Start With Why*, is in no way a book written for spiritual or religious purposes, I believe there is direct application for Christians. If every Christian would come to work with a mindset that the Great Commission is the "why" of their workplace existence, I believe our time at work would be much more awe-inspiring and stimulating.

Christian, are you only concerned about the *how* and *what* of your workplace endeavors, or have you purposed in your heart to make preaching, teaching, discipling, and demonstrating obedience unto the Lord your top priority? Is the Great Commission the "why" of your workplace existence? Are you winning souls and leaving your Christian markers on others? This would be a wonderful beginning for the first mindset change.

POST-IT NOTES

Let's assume that, every time you did something that honored the Lord in the workplace, it would be like leaving a Post-It note on someone you encountered. Every one-on-one conversation with fellow employees, performance review with your boss, and project deliverable that you were asked to produce was like sticking a Post-It note on the individuals involved. It would be like leaving your Christian markers on as many people as you possibly could during the workday.

How are you currently doing? How many of the yellow Post-It notes would be seen in your work environment? What a great way to praise the Lord and shout to the world that your Christian testimony is important to you. Do you think this second mindset change could impact your workplace?

ORGANIZATIONAL INSIGHT

What if we could see all of the elements of organizational and marketplace life through the filter of God's Word? What if our interactions, attitudes, how we handle performance reviews, planning, training, strategy, and our overall approach to communication were laid out before us? Would that change your mindset while at work? What if the basis for all of our decisions and interactions was founded on the Word of God?

We should have the resolve and the depth of character to exude and illuminate the radiance of a Christ-filled and Spirit-led marketplace existence. Here is a list of a few Bible verses that should help us on our way:

> **Listening and communication**: "A fool uttereth all his mind: but a wise man keepeth it in till afterward." (Prov. 29:11)

> **Emotional intelligence**: "The discretion of a man deferreth his anger; and it is his glory to pass over a transgression." (Prov. 19:11)

> **Performance reviews**: "For the commandment is a lamp; and the law is light; and reproofs of instruction are the way of life." (Prov. 6:23)

> **Positive attitude**: "In everything give thanks: for this is the will of God in Christ Jesus concerning you." (1 Thess. 5:18)

Joyful spirit: "Thou wilt keep him in perfect peace, whose mind is stayed on thee: because he trusteth in thee." (Isa. 26:3)

Mentoring: "Where no counsel is, the people fall: but in the multitude of counselors there is safety." (Prov. 11:14)

Communication strategy: "Let no corrupt communication proceed out of your mouth, but that which is good to the use of edifying, that it may minister grace unto the hearers." (Eph. 4:29)

Planning and strategy: "Every purpose is established by counsel: and with good advice make war." (Prov. 20:18)

Trust and faith: "Be merciful unto me, O God, be merciful unto me: for my soul trusteth in thee: yea, in the shadow of thy wings will I make my refuge, until these calamities be overpast." (Psa. 57:1)

Do you have any other verses you can think of that we can add to the list above?

BUILDING A CULTURE

Based on some of the verses listed above, let's now put together a high-level vision of what a Christ-centered culture would look like in today's vernacular. The strategic imperatives should include the following: partnership, teamwork, creativity, joy, dependability, integrity, and excellence. Great organizations should be purpose-driven, performance-oriented, and Bible-led. That is our ultimate lens of responsibility in the workplace.

CHRISTIAN LEADERSHIP WORLDVIEW: PRINCIPLE #3

When we allow the Great Commission to become our workplace inspiration, we will be driven to help create and sustain a culture that is
pleasing to the Lord. We do this by leaving our Christian markers on
everything and everyone we touch or come in contact with along with a
mindset that is creatively different from the world. Only then will we
begin to see the workplace as a cultural manifestation given to us by God
for our stewardship responsibility.

---

[1] Simon Sinek, *Start With Why: How Great Leaders Inspire Everyone to Take Action* (London: Penguin Books Ltd, 2009).

[2] Ibid.

Part 2

THE AUTHORITY TO LEAD

4

OUR PROXY

Christian Leadership: The thoughts, desires, passions, and actions of Christian men and women, by the leading of the Holy Spirit and under God's control, for selfless ends.

Proxy: Power or authority that is given to allow a person to act for someone else.[1]

My prayer for Christians around the world is for them to hold their heads high while at work as they move full-steam ahead. We must be absolutely steadfast in our Christian calling to spread the good news of the gospel message in every imaginable way. Great Christian leaders of the past have voiced a similar resolve. C.H. Spurgeon, A.W. Tozer, John Bunyan, and others have indicated in one form or another that we should use every means possible to further the message of Christ. I believe that their individual pleas have direct application to the workplace. Their heartfelt cries for believers to stand up and lead doesn't originate from human intellect or man-made sentiments. No, their passion to lead stems from the wisdom of the eternal, an understanding so unsearchable and unknowing that it is beyond the understanding of man. The Bible says,

> For my thoughts are not your thoughts, neither are your ways my ways, saith the LORD. (Isa. 55:8)

Yet, God in His infinite wisdom has taken time to write down what His expectations are for Christian leaders. He wants us to be sure of His expectations for us to lead in ways that the world will not comprehend. He wants us to lead with a form of leadership that is paradoxical and goes against every ounce of human knowledge and understanding. Our Lord and Savior, Jesus Christ, wants us to serve and lead with a compassion and concern for others before ourselves.

God set the stage at the beginning of time to communicate unequivocally these leadership expectations by detailing our God-given authority. He told us that He wants us to lead and then set down the exact leadership parameters for how we should go about fulfilling His promise and vision for the Church.

Four primary verses will help us to think through our leadership responsibility areas. These verses contain action-oriented words that quickly help frame our directives from God's Word. They also contain plain speaking directives that we can all embrace. Thank you, Lord, for the simplicity of Your Word!

OUR CHRISTIAN DIRECTIVES

Dominion: Sovereign or supreme authority; the power of governing and controlling.[2]

No effective teaching on Christian leadership can take place without a discussion of our dominion responsibilities. Early in the *Genesis* account of Creation, God laid out a plan for man to exert influence, persuasion, impact, and control. He was telling mankind that we were going to be the vessels and instruments for Him to accomplish His will. If we could only understand the weight of that calling and spiritual assignment! It is an unfathomable blessing from above!

> And God blessed them, and God said unto them, Be fruitful and multiply, and replenish the earth, and subdue it: and have **dominion** over the fish of the sea, and over the

fowl of the air, and over every living thing that moveth
upon the earth. (Gen. 1:28)

God wants man, who was made in His image, to bring glory to
Himself! He does this by assigning a function of leadership through the
Bible. Those dominion responsibilities continue to this day. It is a complete and authoritative directive to influence and subdue the earth.
There was and is much to be done, and having dominion over various
aspects of our existence is a good proving and trying ground for all of
mankind. I also believe that marketplace (workplace) Christians have
been given the authority to rule and impact the businesses, industries,
and people they interact with while at work.

Ambassador: An official envoy; especially : a diplomatic agent of the
highest rank accredited to a foreign government or sovereign as the resident representative of his or her own government or sovereign or
appointed for a special and often temporary diplomatic assignment.[3]

How appropriate is this *Merriam-Webster's* definition of the word *ambassador* above? We are diplomats of the highest rank (made in the image
of God – Genesis 1:27); accredited to a foreign government or sovereign
as the resident representative of his or her own government or sovereign
(we have received the Spirit of adoption from our sovereign Lord – Romans 8:15); or appointed for a special and often temporary diplomatic
assignment (passing our time of sojourning with fear – 1 Peter 1:17).
Yes, we have an official duty to glorify God and proclaim the name of
Jesus Christ.

> Now then we are ambassadors for Christ, as though God
> did beseech you by us: we pray you in Christ's stead, be ye
> reconciled to God. (2 Cor. 5:20)

Does it get any better than that? Wow! God tells us that we have
ambassadorship responsibilities for Christ! The Pharisees and intellectuals of our day want to cloud and confuse our judgment with unending

rabbit trails of theological discussion and debate. If only we could get them to camp on our ambassadorship responsibilities for a while. It helps to simplify and clarify our Christian leadership responsibilities.

God chose Christians to dwell for a short time on Earth before we take up residence in our eternal heavenly home. Being an ambassador is another assumed role and responsibility area that is full of the action and influence of leadership. As ambassadors, we are assigned with the heavenly weight of being Christ's official representative and accredited diplomat. This position is one we must not take lightly. If we are truly going to represent the righteous and holy nature of God Himself, we must be disciplined enough to seek His divine instructions from the Word of God. Our ambassadorship responsibilities will be of no effect if we are not both consumed and conversant in the knowledge, power, and authority of the One who sent us.

Steward: One who actively directs affairs.[4]

The Word of God tells us to be faithful stewards. I love when the Bible makes it crystal clear what we are expected to do. Our stewardship obligations go well beyond the depths of mediocrity and passivity. God expects "that a man be found faithful." The word *faithful* contains overtures of fidelity, honesty, justice, and dependability that we are expected to practice in our daily Christian living. When we combine the two words, *steward* and *faithful,* we begin to understand the enormous leadership assignment we have been given.

> Let a man so account of us, as of the ministers of Christ, and stewards of the mysteries of God. Moreover it is required in stewards, that a man be found faithful. (1 Cor. 4:1-2)

Matthew Henry sums it up best in his commentary.

> The stewards in Christ's family must appoint what he hath appointed. They must not set their fellow-servants to work

for themselves. They must not require anything from them without their Master's warrant. They must not feed them with the chaff of their own inventions, instead of the wholesome food of Christian doctrine and truth. They must teach what he hath commanded, and not the doctrines and commandments of men. They must be true to the interest of their Lord, and consult his honor. The ministers of Christ should make it their hearty and continual endeavor to approve themselves trustworthy; and when they have the testimony of a good conscience, and the approbation of their Master, they must slight the opinions and the censures of their fellow servants.[5]

Power: Possession of control, authority, or influence over others.[6]

God will never assign to us a function of responsibility without first giving to us the associated tools to accomplish His objectives. It would be contrary to His nature. God is not the author of confusion (1 Cor. 14:33). The means that He uses to accomplish His will is the Spirit of God. As believers, we have been given power to impact the world. When we seek the righteous and holy nature of our Lord, we will be endued with wisdom from on high (Holy Spirit) to be able to navigate our leadership responsibilities.

> But ye shall receive power, after that the Holy Ghost is come upon you: and ye shall be witnesses unto me both in Jerusalem, and in all Judaea, and in Samaria, and unto the uttermost part of the earth. (Acts 1:8)

This is just one exhilarating aspect of the many components that make up the life of a Christian leader. God will give to us the associated power (the Comforter) to influence the world. Jesus said,

> Nevertheless I tell you the truth; It is expedient for you that I go away: for if I go not away, the Comforter will not come

unto you; but if I depart, I will send him unto you. (John 16:7)

We have just explored four Christian directives that I pray will help to shape our *Christian leadership worldview*. These Bible truths should give to us great comfort and joy as we serve the Lord. Leadership will not always be an easy road to follow. However, if we rest in the wisdom of His Word, our yokes will be easy and our burdens light (Matt. 11:30).

CHRISTIAN LEADERSHIP WORLDVIEW: PRINCIPLE #4

The word *Christian* should be synonymous with the words *leadership* and *activism*. History is moving forward on the spiritual continuum of God's creation with Christians leading the way. They lead because they decide to fall prostrate before God and are obedient to His directives found in the Bible. Our dominion, ambassadorship, and stewardship responsibilities—along with the power we receive from above—will chart the course of our lives.

[1] www.merriam-webster.com/dictionary/proxy

[2] www.av1611.com/kjv-dictionary/dominion

[3] www.merriam-webster.com/dictionary/ambassador

[4] www.merriam-webster.com/dictionary/steward

[5] *Matthew Henry's Commentary on the Whole Bible, Complete and UNABRIDGED* (Hendrickson Publishers, Inc., 1991).

[6] www.merriam-webster.com/dictionary/power

5

SPIRITUAL GIFTS

*Throughout our lives, God's grace bestows temporal blessings
and spiritual gifts that magnify our abilities and enrich our
lives. His grace refines us. His grace helps us become our best
selves.*

—DIETER F. UCHTDORF

In the previous chapter, we examined various directives the Bible
gives to highlight our authority (proxy) to lead. I indicated that one
of the directives included receiving power from the Holy Spirit to
act according to His will and get things done. We need to take this
Christian doctrine one step further. We need to ask ourselves, "How
does God manifest the Holy Spirit in our day-to-day leadership responsibilities?" He does so through our spiritual gifts and natural talents.

As I've traveled and taught on the subject of Christian leadership,
I have been taken aback by how uncomfortable Christians are talking
about their spiritual gifts. On rare occasions, someone will raise his/her
hand and give an explicit and detailed answer about his spiritual gift(s)
or God-given natural abilities, but that is not generally the case. Christians are not decisive when they are asked to talk about their spiritual
gifts. Using our spiritual gifts and natural talents are critical to making
an impact for the Kingdom of God, and we must not shy away from
them. We should not be hesitant to talk openly about the gifts God has
given to us.

We don't recognize our gifts in a way that brings undue and un-
warranted attention to ourselves. No, we talk about spiritual gifts and

natural talents as a way to give glory to His name. I believe that, when spiritual gifts and natural talents are openly discussed, this will bring a higher sense of accountability to exercise those gifts and get the Body of Christ on board with specific involvement.

The following outline is a brief attempt to organize various sources of Bible information to help us understand our spiritual gifts and the corresponding responsibilities. These responsibilities help frame our authority (proxy) to lead and exert influence on society. Much of the information below is taken from the *King James Study Bible*.

ENABLING GIFTS

These gifts are foundational to the basic Christian belief system and are given to all Christians in varying degrees and intensity. They include the following:

- Faith (Rom. 1:11; 1 Cor. 12:9)
- Knowledge (1 Cor. 12:8)
- Wisdom (1 Cor. 12:8)
- Discernment (1 Cor. 12:10)[1]

These gifts help Christians to develop and use their motivational gifts more fully (listed below). They are collaborative in nature, building and strengthening one another for the edification of believers. In a sense, they have a unifying and bonding compound that ignites the power of the Holy Spirit.

MOTIVATIONAL GIFTS

These are task-oriented gifts that are unique to the believer and for the edification of the Church Body. They include the following:

- Prophecy (Rom. 12:6; 1 Cor. 14:3)
- Teaching (Rom. 12:7)
- Exhortation (Rom. 12:8)

- Shepherding (Eph. 4:11)
- Mercy (Rom. 12:8)
- Ministering (Rom. 12:7)
- Helping (1 Cor. 12:28)
- Giving (Rom. 12:8)
- Ruling (Rom. 12:8)
- Governing (1 Cor. 12:28)
- Evangelism (Eph. 4:11)
- Hospitality (1 Pet. 4:9)[2]

Now that we have explored some of the components of both enabling and motivational gifts, let's look at some of the nuances of our spiritual gifts and how the Lord organizes them for maximum effectiveness.

First, we see the great diversity that we have in the Body of Christ. When the power of that diversity is unleashed, it is impossible to stop. Spiritual wonders in high places will take root and be wonderfully illuminated.

> Now there are diversities of gifts, but the same spirit. And there are differences of administrations, but the same Lord. And there are diversities of operations, but it is the same God which worketh all in all. (1 Cor. 12:4-6)

God confers both spiritual gifts and natural talents on man for the good of the Church, others, and His glory. As Christians, we have been given spiritual gifts from God to provide a deeper understanding and spiritual consciousness in specific areas. These gifts have been illuminated in special and unique ways. Why "illuminated", you ask? So we can share an awareness of the glory of God with those we come in contact with and proclaim the name of Jesus.

Spiritual gifts are given to us by the Spirit of God once we have been saved. They blossom as we mature in our faith and are used to glorify God as we serve others and build up the family of God.

On the other hand, natural talents are the result of our genetic inheritance and the training we receive from our family environment. They are possessed by both believers and non-believers, and they can be used to serve God or to serve ourselves. God's ultimate desire is for the body of Christ to be blessed, edified, and to walk away with a deeper awareness and understanding in spiritual matters.

> But the manifestation of the Spirit is given to every man to profit withal. (1 Cor. 12:7)

God has raised the expectations of behavior and performance of Christians to another level upon acceptance of Christ as Savior. We have a duty to make sure that other Christians are profiting spiritually from our gifts. I believe that God will extract our maximum leadership potential by putting us in positions where we don't think we can handle our leadership responsibilities. When we sit back and reflect on the various growth experiences in life, we can reasonably deduce that leadership is hard work. Leading from the front can potentially be uncomfortable and difficult.

I am sure that each of us can think back over the years to at least one point when God has given to us a "stretch assignment." It may not have been pleasant, but it helped us to grow as believers and to make an impact on others for the glory of God. Another way to say it is that God puts us out of our leadership "comfort zones" so we will learn to trust Him more. With each experience, God blesses us and expands our capacity to lead others for His own glory. We must also realize that there is a uniqueness to our spiritual gifts.

> Now ye are the body of Christ, and members in particular. (1 Cor. 12:27)

This verse is telling us that we have a specific calling and duty to perform relating to our gifts. When we are all leading through the use of our spiritual gifts and natural talents for the glory of God, it puts God's Church in "alignment" and in perfect balance and harmony to influence our culture. Just think of the enabling power that might be derived from the teamwork and unity demonstrated when the optimal alignment is achieved. It would be breathtaking.

Not only does God tell us to lead with our dominionship, ambassadorship, and stewardship credentials, He gives to us the power (Holy Spirit) along with the unique and specific skill sets (spiritual and natural gifts) to accomplish His will for the Church.

On top of this, He gives to us a resting and hiding place when things begin to go sideways. It is a fault-tolerant and closed-loop process of spiritual growth, heavenly determination, and unmitigated rest that will steer the course of life, assuming the instruction manual (Bible) is consistently read and heeded. The Bible is a perfect model of leadership focused on spiritual growth that glorifies God and helps the believer to grow into the image of God Himself.

CHRISTIAN LEADERSHIP WORLDVIEW: PRINCIPLE #5

When Christian leaders place their spiritual gifts at the feet of the Master, give the glory to God, and are obedient to His will, they impact the world. When we empty ourselves of ourselves and build others up, we exhibit true Christian leadership. It's paradoxical but true! How are you using your spiritual gifts and natural talents for the Lord in the workplace?

---

[1] *King James Study Bible* (previously published as *The Liberty Annotated Study Bible* and as *The Annotated Study Bible*, King James Version, 1988 by Liberty University).

[2] Ibid.

6

A Concern for Others

One of the things that makes our military the best in the world is the certain knowledge of each Soldier, Sailor, Airman, and Marine that they can always count on their comrades should they need help—*that* they will never be abandoned.

—Jon Kyl

s I began writing this chapter of the book, I realized I could not get the words *Marine Corps* out of my head. Each time I would sit down to write, my mind would start to wander and begin to focus and meditate on what it means to be a Marine. I am sure that the recent death of my uncle (Steve Reny) just a few days before I started writing this book had something to do with it. I have been thinking about my Aunt Sandra and praying that the upcoming funeral would stir the hearts of believers and nonbelievers alike.

Uncle Steve was a dedicated Marine on the front lines in Vietnam who willingly sacrificed all he had for his country. During one of his tours, he was shot in the head and left for dead. By the grace of God, someone noticed that he was still alive and loaded him on a truck that took him to a military hospital. After a lengthy recovery, he went on to live a wonderful and meaningful life for the Lord. Uncle Steve risked his life for the good of others.

My thoughts about the Marine Corps may also have been related to the many conversations I've had with my second son (Kyle) about his leadership training while he served as an officer in the Marines Corps.

The Marines place a high premium on taking care of their fellow Marines. Kyle and my Uncle Steve led me to do a little more digging about what the Marine Corps is all about.

In an article that was published in September of 1995, General C.C. Krulak related a story about what Marines do and what they don't do. In one portion of the article he asks, "What do Marines do?" He then goes on to list a few of his thoughts.

- Marines do – maintain their bearing.
- Marines do – more with less.
- Marines do – strive to improve themselves physically, tactically, intellectually.
- Marines do – honor their word.
- Marines do – set the example.
- Marines do – take the initiative.
- Marines do – remain loyal to their families, fellow Marines, the Corps, and the Nation.
- Marines do – respect each other.
- Marines do – take care of each other.
- Marines do – what's right.[1]

This list of what Marines are expected to do is a tall task to execute. I believe that most Marines strive to live out each of these statements with the core of their being. What caught my eye in General Krulak's article were the last four items in the list. Remaining loyal, respecting, taking care of, and doing what is right for each other are callings of the highest order. They fit perfectly into what I want to convey about Christian leadership in the workplace.

As leaders, our authority must be pointed toward a concern for other people. If we are not careful, we could all go through life with a selfish concern for ourselves and with little-to-no room for a servant leader's sacrificial love.

Let's now consider the heroic efforts of another Marine and how his concern for others (like my Uncle Steve) made a difference.

On June 19, Cpl. Kyle Carpenter became only the second living Marine to receive the nation's highest military award for valor, the Medal of Honor, for heroic actions in the global war on terrorism. During a firefight in Afghanistan in 2010, the then 21-year-old lance corporal threw himself on a Taliban grenade to protect another Marine, Lance Cpl. Nicholas Eufrazio. Both men were seriously wounded by the blast. It's a miracle that Carpenter, now medically retired, is even alive to receive the medal. Of the 13 Medals of Honor earned in Iraq and Afghanistan since 2001, four went to service members who threw themselves on a grenade to save others. Carpenter is the only one of the four to survive such a selfless act. And only the quick actions of his fellow Marines and the incredible efforts of U.S. military medical personnel kept his grievous wounds from being fatal too.[2]

As I read this beautiful account of selflessness, I think of my Savior. I believe that Jesus was the epitome of servant leadership and selflessness. He knew He would have to shed His blood on the cross of Calvary for the sins of mankind. He also knew He would suffer an indescribable agony and death as our substitute on the cross. Yet, He was willing!

And being in an agony he prayed more earnestly: and his sweat was as it were great drops of blood falling down to the ground. (Luke 22:44)

Yes, Jesus was willing to pay it all because He had a concern for others. While this example of the ultimate sacrifice tugs at our heart strings, there are numerous other verses that point to His selfless concern for others as well.

And Jesus went forth, and saw a great multitude, and was moved with compassion toward them, and he healed their sick. (Matt. 14:14)

Christ went. He was moved toward something so He could make an impact and make a difference.

Christ saw. He saw the multitude and the great need because he was willing (yielded) to be among the multitude.

Christ was moved. The Holy Spirit was evident in that He was moved with compassion.

Christ acted. He was compelled and burdened to act.

Christian leaders in the workplace should be driven and compelled to move *toward* organizational needs. When we spot an opportunity to make a difference at work, we need to seize the opportunity. Christians should be on the lookout for situations where we can lend a helping hand to those in need. Having a concern for other people in the workplace should be a Christian leader's top priority. We do so because we have a spiritual understanding and compassion that drives us forward. There are no thoughts of self-promotion or prominence but rather a recognition that we have a Christian duty to take action that helps further define and highlight our relationship with Christ. We do not take action to differentiate ourselves from fellow employees by comparing our checklist of workplace activities and initiatives against others. No, our motivation should be spiritual in nature and not tainted with the designs of this world.

Our responsibility to proclaim the name of Jesus should go well beyond our verbalization of the gospel message. Our co-workers expect to see a difference in how we conduct ourselves and live out our faith while at work. They expect us to take action when a need arises.

When was the last time you went the extra mile in the workplace? Can you immediately bring to mind a situation in which you went above and beyond the call of duty?

We must never forget the dynamics of our responsibilities. Workplace leadership is relational and involves human interaction. It encompasses elements of persuasion while exhibiting the highest levels of collaboration, teamwork, trust, and love. Christians should be driven by the highest form of love in the workplace. *Agape* love is the ultimate form of love known to mankind. It is a love that is free from the isolation of human emotion and desire. Agape love is driven by a sense of duty, responsibility, and Spirit-led desire that only God himself could design. It is a self-sacrificing love that drove Jesus to the cross of Calvary. I pray that our Christian leadership in the workplace will demonstrate the same self-sacrificing love that is focused on a concern for others.

CHRISTIAN LEADERSHIP WORLDVIEW: PRINCIPLE #6

There is no higher calling in the workplace than to impact others for the glory of the Lord. We become true leaders when we move beyond the confines of self by jumping into the spiritual realm of self-sacrifice and an uncommon love for others. And while we may never have to jump on a grenade for our co-workers, we do have a responsibility as employees to shroud our workplace environment with the spiritual provision and protection given to us from above.

---

[1] www.MCA-Marines.org/leatherneck/message-commandment-marines-dont-do

[2] www.forbes.com/sites/donesmond/2014/11/13/marines-take-care-of-marines

7

CHRISTIAN ACTIVISM

Leadership is not about a title or a designation. It's about impact, influence and inspiration. Impact involves getting results, influence is about spreading the passion you have for your work, and you have to inspire team-mates and customers.

—ROBIN S. SHARMA

We are only beginning to scratch the surface of the evangelistic goldmine found in the workplace arena. Moving forward, Christians need to engage the enemy fully so we can first take and then hold the spiritual high ground in the workplace environment.

As I think back over the 33 years I was in the corporate world, I am disappointed to report that I can count on two hands the number of times Christians identified themselves as believers either with their words or their actions. In other words, I couldn't tell that they were Bible-believing Christians. For whatever reason, Christians in today's workforce are satisfied with flying under the radar screen, getting along, not rocking the boat, and collecting a paycheck. Often, even the traditional noon-day prayer is put on the shelf for fear of appearing to be too much of an evangelical Christian!

In this chapter, we'll explore what is happening, why it is happening, and what we can do (activism) to bring hope and change to the workplace domain.

WHAT IS HAPPENING?

Christians are being lured into accepting a redefinition of Christian morality and ethics. In many organizations across America, we are being bullied into accepting moral standards that are not our own. These organizations are propagating and enacting a moral code of ethics and standards that are not found in the Bible. They are trying to codify a belief system that wreaks with the stench of Hades. Christians everywhere are being bullied into accepting the doctrines of the Secular Humanist religion or to suffer the consequences. Those consequences may be subtle by hiding themselves behind the lack of upward mobility or by presenting themselves with outright hostility through censure, legal proceedings, and/or loss of employment. This organizational indoctrination hits on and encroaches a variety of sacred and valued Christian beliefs. A few of those valued Christian beliefs are described below.

- Marriage is between a man and a woman.
- Gender is determined at birth through existing DNA and natural (God-given) physical genetics.
- Absolute truth stems from and originates in God's Word.
- Truth is not relative or man-made. Truth is divine.
- Man has an Adamic sin nature and was born inherently evil.
- Man needs to repent and receive Christ as Savior for eternal life and redemption.
- God is sovereign.

WHY IS IT HAPPENING?

Many of our workplace institutions have become adept at drowning out our Christian voices with rules, regulations, and man-made laws that are anti-God. This type of workplace governance (control) is surely designed to limit both the depth and breadth of Christian influence and impact. Over time, they want to silence and eliminate all traces of Christianity in the workplace.

The enemy has cleverly designed a way to stifle our voices at work with a strategy that is a backdoor human resources approach. This approach is called "sensitivity training." This form of Secular Humanist training comes in many different forms. The unbelieving world won't necessarily take notice that the strategy is trying to undermine the foundational principles of ethical and moral behavior found in God's Word. The world simply sees this "sensitivity training" and strategy as a way to be polite, respectful, and inclusive of everything and everyone. They simply don't want to offend.

Most unsuspecting nonbelievers naively believe that they have no "skin in the game" for Christian ethical and moral standards found in Biblical instruction and that they don't have to worry. On the other hand, we have suspecting Christians who know and understand exactly what is happening but feel so overwhelmed, threatened, and helpless that they don't know what to do or how to respond. Day after day, Christians come to work experiencing the onslaught of religious persecution while cowering for workplace survival.

The third player we have in this realm of organizational life is Satan. He is the master strategist and enemy (along with his minions) who is manipulating the chess pieces for his ultimate gain and control.

What do I mean when I refer to the enemy's strategy as a *backdoor human resource approach*? The enemy is wise enough to know that America still has a significant number of believers who would not stand for a direct and all-out frontal assault on our faith. At this point in American history, Christians would cry foul if there was direct persecution for being and identifying as a Christian while at work. In other words, we are not at a point where Christians are overtly and broadly being denied workplace equalities based on our faith. Yes, we do have many examples of this rearing its ugly head; I understand that. However, for the most part, these are still isolated instances. So, instead of employers saying, "We don't hire Christians," Satan has devised a way through the back door to assault us with three primary strategic maneuvers.

1: Stifled Christian Voices

By suggesting and presenting an alternative view of the workplace (Secular Humanism) and by making those views (doctrines) off-limits to debate or modification, the enemy keeps control, drives the narrative, and codifies a belief system in organizational life not shared by Christians. The belief system then becomes part of the rules, regulations, processes, and ultimately the organizational culture. I think we could agree that changing a culture is hard work—if it can be changed at all. This alternative worldview has the effect of stifling our Christian voices and boldness to share the gospel message of Christ. It keeps us on the outside looking in.

2: Change through Conditioning

Time can be an enemy for Christians when considering our basic human weaknesses. Satan knows that, over time, many well-intentioned Christians in the workplace will become numb and conditioned to the ways of the world. Often, we get sucked into the world's ways of thinking by rationalizing, justifying, and then defending small deviations from the absolute truth of God's Word. Before you know it, a decade or two will have passed with our consciences still void of any particular sense of righteous indignation for moral and ethical issues that would have previously roiled our spiritual sensitivities. If you don't think this statement is true, just think back to a few decades ago and consider what society thought about the primary social issues of our time (current day). Without firm action and a plan to take an offensive position at work, I believe that the continuum of time will be our enemy.

3: Guerilla Warfare

The enemy is using a guerilla-warfare approach to attacking our faith. He hits us hard, disappears into the landscape, and then regroups for another attack with uncanny stealth. The enemy is hoping to win a number of small battles that will eventually compound into a decisive victory.

He wants us to stay focused on the small and incremental gains he can make without anyone noticing or caring. He would be happy to fly under the radar if that meant he could twist and denigrate the authority of God's Word.

WHAT CAN WE DO?

First, we must be active participants in workplace governance and culture building. We should never sit on the sidelines of organizational life and "catch" the enemy's 100-mile-per-hour fastballs headed our way. Christians will either stand up, get involved, and cause change, or the enemy will.

Generally speaking, human beings want to be led by something or someone. They want to unite behind leaders who can articulate the hope of a brighter tomorrow. They want leaders and leadership principles that point to a future that is mighty and significant in nature. We all desire to be part of something unique and special. It is our Christian duty to make sure our coworkers are pointed in the right spiritual direction.

Second, we should always be concerned about the small encroachments on the Kingdom of God. We should never be satisfied or allow heretical advances by the enemy, regardless of the size. Speak out when you see inconsistencies relating to the truth of God's Word.

Third, we must be diligent prayer warriors for *every* aspect of the workplace environment. Nothing should be off-limits for our prayer consideration. As identified in the introduction of this book, the workplace is of significant value to our Lord. He wants to hear the heartfelt cries from His children relating to workplace demands. Christ wants the marketplace to be a thriving Christian experience where we take charge and lead!

CHRISTIAN LEADERSHIP WORLDVIEW – PRINCIPLE #7

Sitting idly by at work should never be an option for Christians. That kind of inaction plays right into the enemy's hands. We must defend our faith in our Lord and Savior, Jesus Christ, while at work. Christian activism will help to stem the tide and dampen the advances of the enemy. More positively stated, Christian activism will bring the needed light and salt to preserve and protect our Christian workplace freedoms.

Part 3

THE SOURCE AND ESSENCE OF LEADERSHIP

8

GOD'S WORD

Christian marketplace leaders must have a personal knowledge of God's character while consistently demonstrating the fruits thereof.

B ible-believing Christians have been taught that Jesus Christ is both the incarnate and inspired Word of God. As a result of this teaching, we have learned that one of the ways He chose to reveal Himself to man was through His Word.

> In the beginning was the Word, and the Word was with God, and the Word was God. (John 1:1)

The blessed gift of His Word is the source and essence from which all good things flow. This includes our leadership responsibilities.

Jesus chose to live among humans for approximately 33 years and for people to get to know Him on a deep and personal level. As our Creator who made us in the image of God, He wanted to make sure that we have ample resources necessary to discern and then imitate the holy and righteous nature of our Lord. He has never been interested in Christians acting out, creating, or engineering worldly thoughts and man-made machinations of what they think to be holy and right. God so loved the world that He gave us everything we need in His Word in order to reflect His righteous nature.

The old sin nature of man remains determined to produce some new "creative genius" so that humanity can take all of the honor and glory. The world loves to focus on what man can do to "fix" war, poverty, crime, hunger, drinking water, disease, and more. By doing so, the world believes it can help to bring the focus, prominence, and the goodness of man to the forefront. God simply wants us to reflect on and live out the Christian faith that has already been established in His Word. He doesn't want any pretense, false humility, or pride. He wants us to focus on Him and His Word.

> And the Word was made flesh, and dwelt among us, (and we beheld his glory, the glory as of the only begotten of the Father,) full of grace and truth. (John 1:14)

The Savior of the world lived among men and exhibited unmerited favor toward His children in a manner that depicted absolute truth and righteousness. He was fully God and fully man. His willingness to experience humanity and then die on the cross for the sins of the world is all we need to know about His leadership style and moral character. His character begins and ends with a deep love for His children. All He expects is for us to reciprocate that love back to Him by believing in His Son, Jesus Christ. This seems to be a small price to pay for the blessings and spiritual riches we have been afforded here on Earth.

> For of him, and through him, and to him, are all things: to whom be glory for ever. Amen. (Rom. 11:36)

We know that God is the source of all things ("of Him"). He is the source from which all things flow that will shape our spiritual and moral character and give to us the ability to lead ("through Him"). God should also be the focal point and center of our earthly existence ("to Him") as we give to Him the respect, reverence, and glory that He deserves ("to whom be glory for ever. Amen.").

We have also been taught as Bible-believing Christians that His Word is supernatural and beyond human understanding. Let's take a look at some of the words that describe the Bible's majesty.

Visionary

Where there is no vision, the people perish: but he that keepeth the law, happy is he. (Prov. 28:18)

God casts a vision for His people through divine revelation from His Word.

God-breathed

All scripture is given by inspiration of God, and is profitable for doctrine, for reproof, for correction, for instruction in righteousness. (2 Tim. 3:16)

Verbally-inspired

But I certify you, brethren, that the gospel which was preached of me is not after man. For I neither received it of man, neither was I taught it, but by the revelation of Jesus Christ. (Gal. 1:11-12)

Inerrant

For verily I say unto you, Till heaven and earth pass, one jot or one tittle shall in no wise pass from the law, till all be fulfilled. (Matt. 5:18)

Indestructible

The grass withereth, the flower fadeth: but the word of our God shall stand for ever. (Isa. 40:8)

Infallible

> We have also a more sure word of prophecy; whereunto ye do well that ye take heed, as unto a light that shineth in a dark place, until the day dawn, and the day star arise in your hearts: Knowing this first, that no prophecy of the scripture is of any private interpretation. For the prophecy came not in old time by the will of man: but holy men of God spake as they were moved by the Holy Ghost. (2 Pet. 1:19-21)

Eternal

> For ever, O LORD, thy word is settled in heaven.
> (Psa. 119:89)

What a privilege it is for Christian leaders to be able to look in the Bible and take comfort that "all things leadership" can be found. The inspired Word of God is the most perfect leadership manual in every conceivable way. I believe that the highest model of leadership has been determined since the foundation of the world. God has revealed that model of leadership in His Word. In the very beginning, wisdom charted her course for the holy and righteous nature of Christian leadership to exist. When we become a child of God and diligently seek the Scriptures, we learn and discover (progressive sanctification) what it means to be true Christian leaders.

CHRISTIAN LEADERSHIP WORLDVIEW: PRINCIPLE #8

The Bible is the source of what it means to be a leader. The world continues to work hard at developing revolutionary and innovative leadership models that can change the world. Month after month, leading publications offer their version of the latest and greatest in leadership theory. Outside of some technical jargon or reframed concepts, I have never found any worthy leadership concepts that can't be traced to God's Word. He is the Alpha and Omega! Praise God!

9

GOD'S CHARACTER REVEALED

*Faith is deliberate confidence in the character of God whose
ways you may not understand at the time.*

—OSWALD CHAMBERS

As we transition from the old life of imputed sin and iniquity to
our new life imputed with the righteousness of Christ, we
should painstakingly study the Scriptures to find the higher and
more perfect way. The habitual, careful, and thoughtful examination of
God's Word will help to lead us into a deep understanding of God's
character. Both His moral character and divine nature must be explored.

GOD'S MORAL CHARACTER

If we have come to the conclusion beyond the shadow of a doubt that
God is who He says He is, we have no other choice but to desperately
seek and then to identify with His moral attributes. Accordingly, logic
would tell us that every aspect of His revealed moral character must be
pursued with a holy fervor and discipline like no other. The more we
know about Him and His ways, the more pliable and moldable we will
become as leaders who are filled with the Holy Spirit. While all 66 books
of the Bible are an appropriate catalog for such a pursuit, the book of
Galatians is a wonderful place to start. We would be remiss if we did not
begin with the fruit of the Spirit as part of these foundational leadership
truths. The following leadership characteristics are all interrelated and
nourish one another, complement one another, and have the effect of

building upon one another. Any effective study of Christian leadership must include the fruit of the Spirit.

> But the fruit of the Spirit is love, joy, peace, long-suffering, gentleness, goodness, faith, meekness, temperance: against such there is no law. (Gal. 5:22-23)

The Lord has provided this passage with all of its beauty, rhythm, harmony, and wellspring of godly wisdom for Christian leadership instruction. This passage encompasses such an exponential magnitude of wisdom and knowledge that only God Himself can grasp its full and complete meaning. While our limited intellectual capacity must suffice for now, we should approach each study in the Scriptures with the awe, praise, and worship due His name.

- **Love:** Sacrificial and selfless love (agape); not expecting anything in return
- **Joy:** Gladness of heart; constant delight in God
- **Peace:** Contentment; calmness; having one's emotions balanced and under control
- **Long-suffering:** His patient nature to defer anger; the very close friend of mercy; God withholding (delays) those things that we do actually deserve
- **Gentleness:** Sweetness of temper; the calm sweet sister of compassion; a thoughtful serenity
- **Goodness:** Kindness; a readiness to do good toward others
- **Faithfulness:** Believing and trusting God in spite of circumstances; fidelity, justice, and honesty that we commit and promise to others; an element of being dependable
- **Meekness:** My power under God's control for selfless ends; control of our passions and our resentments

- **Temperance**: The power of self-control through vigilance; part of our ability to exhibit temperance is our ability to "die daily" as the Apostle Paul explains to us; to avoid excessive and immoderate behavior[1]

Beyond the fruit of the Spirit, we must also add things like God's mercy, grace, justice, righteousness, holiness, and truth to the list of His moral characteristics. When I consider the finite portion of God's moral character listed above—He is the Alpha and Omega, and there is so much more—I am struck by how far removed I am from those optimal characteristics. It makes me realize just how wicked and deplorable I really am. I am but the dust of the earth. I have so much growing to do and so little time in which to do it.

What if my heart was full-to-the-brim with those nine fruits of the Spirit? How much more of an effective witness and leader could I be for the Lord Jesus Christ? How much more could He use me here on Earth? Would a humble and contrite heart filled with the righteousness of the fruit of the Spirit overflow into the tributary of grace that leads to the reservoir of leadership? As a leader, could I then walk in liberty while at work, exuding Christ by being filled with His Spirit? Oh, Lord, please create in me a clean heart (Psa. 51:10), for I know that my heart is deceitful above all things and desperately wicked (Jer. 17:9). Help me, dear Lord, to communicate the spiritual needs of the workplace environment.

The Essence of Marketplace Leadership

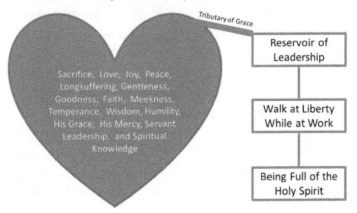

GOD'S DIVINE NATURE

These are the qualities that only God Himself possesses. There are no spiritual powers or forces anywhere that share His divine nature and attributes. They belong to God and to God alone. These qualities define Him as the preeminent being of the universe from whom all blessings, instruction, and wisdom flow. What a privilege it is to serve a risen Savior.

He is eternal.

> How much more shall the blood of Christ, who through the eternal Spirit offered himself without spot to God, purge your conscience from dead works to serve the living God? (Heb. 9:14)

He is omniscient.

> But God hath revealed them unto us by his Spirit: for the Spirit searcheth all things, yea, the deep things of God. (1 Cor. 2:10)

But the Comforter, which is the Holy Ghost, whom the Father will send in my name, he shall teach you all things, and bring all things to your remembrance, whatsoever I have said unto you. (John 14:26)

He is omnipotent.

By his spirit he hath garnished the heavens; his hand hath formed the crooked serpent. (Job 26:13)

And the angel answered and said unto her, The Holy Ghost shall come upon thee, and the power of the Highest shall overshadow thee: therefore also that holy thing which shall be born of thee shall be called the Son of God. And, behold, thy cousin Elisabeth, she hath also conceived a son in her old age: and this is the sixth month with her, who was called barren. For with God nothing shall be impossible. (Luke 1:35-37)

He is omnipresent.

Whither shall I go from thy spirit? or whither shall I flee from thy presence? If I ascend up into heaven, thou art there: if I make my bed in hell, behold, thou art there. If I take the wings of the morning, and dwell in the uttermost parts of the sea; Even there shall thy hand lead me, and thy right hand shall hold me. (Psa. 139:7-10)

He is holy.

It is often forgotten that His name contains one of His important attributes. He is God; therefore, He is holy. It should be remembered always that the One Who is present with us at all times is *holy*.

He is truth.

> This is he that came by water and blood, even Jesus Christ; not by water only, but by water and blood. And it is the Spirit that beareth witness, because the Spirit is truth. (1 John 5:6)

He is life.

> For the law of the Spirit of life in Christ Jesus hath made me free from the law of sin and death. (Rom. 8:2)

He is wisdom.

> Who hath directed the Spirit of the LORD, or being his counsellor hath taught him? (Isaiah 40:13)

He is sovereign.

> But all these worketh that one and the selfsame Spirit, dividing to every man severally as he will. (1 Cor. 12:11)[2]

How can one study the Word of God and not be totally convinced that He is the one true God? Our leadership abilities in the workplace will only mature when we turn from our sinful and pride-filled ways and look to the Lord for guidance. We all know that studying is not enough. We need to put on the new man which God created in righteousness and true holiness (Eph. 4:24).

CHRISTIAN LEADERSHIP WORLDVIEW: PRINCIPLE #9

God's moral character and divine nature must be diligently sought after, understood, and lived out if we are to become true Christian leaders. Head knowledge is simply not enough. The tough part of leadership is in the execution portion. It is only when the Spirit of God fills our souls that we can experience Christian leadership. It's only the unique and mysterious combination of God's sovereignty and man's determined "will" that produces those blessed workplace leadership results.

---

[1] *Matthew Henry's Commentary on the Whole Bible*. Complete and UNABRIDGED (Hendrickson Publishers, Inc., 1991).

[2] Michael C. Bere, *Bible Doctrines for Today*, Second Edition (Pensacola Christian College, 1996).

10

WHAT LEADERSHIP CAN NEVER BE

*Sir, my concern is not whether God is on our side; my greatest
concern is to be on God's side, for God is always right.*

—ABRAHAM LINCOLN

In our discussion so far, it has been repeatedly stated that a proper
understanding of authentic leadership will only be attained when
we are living out Biblical instruction. When we combine our diligent study of His Word with the necessary action, we produce a Christ-
like form of leadership that will span the ages and meet the test of time.
However, any serious student of Christian leadership must also possess
an in-depth awareness of the enemy's strategy and tactics relating to
leadership. Not only should we declare the narrow paths of Christian
leadership through righteous instruction, we also have a responsibility to
warn others when the enemy approaches.

In this chapter, we will explore a form of leadership that doesn't
line up with God's Word. This will help us to discern improper notions
of leadership theory and doctrine and then provide effective leadership
coaching and instruction to believers.

Secular Humanism is one of the most vulgar and egregious forms
of leadership being taught around the world. The leadership theory being spewed blatantly attacks the foundations of the Christian faith with
no apology for teaching that a spiritual domain doesn't exist. The leaders
of the Secular Humanist propaganda machine will boldly articulate a
message of a world void of God, one that places "humanity" front and
center of the universe.

Let's consider the foundational premise of Secular Humanism. Its proponents want us to place our full confidence and eternal existence in man's ability. Their basic premise is that humans can overcome all obstacles.

Let's now take a look at how the enemy is twisting wholesome leadership principles for his own selfish purposes. We need to consider the warning in the book of *Jeremiah*.

> Thus saith the Lord, Let not the wise man glory in *his wisdom*, neither let the mighty man glory in *his might*, let not the rich man glory in *his riches*: But let him that glorieth glory in this, that he understandeth and knoweth me, that I am the Lord which exercise lovingkindness, judgment, and righteousness, in the earth: for in these things I delight, saith the Lord. (Jer. 9:23-24)

We are at a time in our great nation's history when the enemy will do and say anything to further his agenda. All of the rules of yesteryear where righteousness, gentlemanly and womanly behavior, moral authority and precepts, absolute truth, and the decorum of human decency that once prevailed have been replaced with subtlety, lies, and deception. The eruption that we see developing across America has been percolating beneath the surface for some time now. The Secular Humanist strategy along with all the groundwork that its leaders have laid over the years is now starting to take effect. Some would say that the "chicken has come home to roost." Secular Humanism has reached its ugly tentacles deep into the fabric of America's soul and psyche. Fortunately, the strategy and tactics used by the enemy have not gone unnoticed by many of its citizens. However, many are still being fooled and lulled to sleep into an oblivion of acceptance.

There are also many enlightened and God-fearing people in the United States of America who perceive the approaches of Satan and his agenda. Make no mistake; Secular Humanism and all of its derivative forms are the Devil's playpen.

SECULAR HUMANISM DEFINED

The following is a definition of *Secular Humanism*:

> The philosophy or life stance of secular humanism (alternatively known by some adherents as Humanism, specifically with a capital H to distinguish it from other forms of humanism) embraces human reason, ethics, and philosophical naturalism while specifically rejecting religious dogma, supernaturalism, pseudoscience, and superstition as the bases of morality and decision making.[1]

The underlying objectives are clear in a Secular Humanist environment. Its proponents want to elevate the greatness of man over the greatness of God by rejecting any/all forms of faith, spiritual doctrine, and absolute truth (Bible truth).

Let's focus our attention on one particular strategic approach being used by Secular Humanists to confound the masses. Many of our leading institutions of higher education are being used as pawns for the propagation of this strategy. I am talking about the "mirroring" strategy. *Mirroring* is an ingenuous tool being used by our institutions of higher education resulting in devastating consequences to our core values and belief systems. The tool is so basic and childlike that it often goes unnoticed by the general public. In fact, it looks and sounds like a godly concern for the well-being of others while taking our focus away from our Lord and Savior, Jesus Christ.

Wikipedia tells us that *mirroring* is

> ...the behavior in which one person subconsciously imitates the gesture, speech pattern, or attitude of another. Mirroring often occurs in social situations, particularly in the company of close friends or family. The concept often affects other individual's notions about the individual that is exhibiting mirroring behaviors, which can lead to the individual building rapport with others.[2]

So there it is! Satan is trying to build rapport with the world in order to disguise his ulterior motives of encroaching the throne of God. He passionately wants to discredit the one true Alpha and Omega God. We also know that Satan is the master of subtlety and deceit.

> Now the serpent was more subtil than any beast of the field which the LORD God had made. And he said unto the woman, Yea, hath God said, Ye shall not eat of every tree of the garden? (Gen. 3:1)

> And no marvel; for Satan himself is transformed into an angel of light. (2 Cor. 11:14)

Yes, Satan has the ability to make things sound and look like images from Heaven above. He can manipulate the means of accomplishing his agenda through strategic deployment that will tug at the heart strings of human emotions. He can take you on a feel-good emotional journey through mirroring that will make you think you are approaching the divine nature of God himself. Let us now take a look at one of those subtle approaches being used in leadership courses taught at some of the leading colleges and universities across our land.

There are four primary leadership objectives that are being propagated by Secular Humanists in leadership courses that often get overlooked. They go unnoticed because, on the surface, these objectives feel and sound like good things to focus on and achieve. Let's take a close look at each of these objectives and how they relate to Christianity and our society at large.

- Integrity
- Authenticity
- Being part of something that is bigger than yourself
- Having cause in the matter[3]

At first, don't these four objectives give you a warm and fuzzy feeling? At first sight, they seem to be leading to something that is pure, ethical, moral, and selfless. Don't they? But they are not, and here is the reasoning and rationale why this is the case. We'll start with a Christian perspective on the objectives and their traditional historical context and meaning.

TRADITIONAL DEFINITIONS

Integrity: Firm adherence to a code of especially moral or artistic values.[4]

Authenticity: Real or genuine; not copied or false; true and accurate; made to be or look just like an original.[5]

Bigger than yourself: We look to Christ and His Church as the selfless focus and motivation of being part of something bigger than ourselves.

Being cause in the matter: We want to leave Christ's markers on others and proclaim the gospel message as ambassadors for Him while sojourning on Earth. In other words, once we are saved, we want to impact people by being "doers of the word" of God and "not hearers only" (Jas. 1:22).

SECULAR HUMANIST MANIPULATED DEFINITIONS:

Integrity: Many leadership courses being taught attempt to chip away at the foundation of Christian values and standards. I call this the "divide-and-conquer" approach. The leadership models being used in many of the courses presuppose a definition of integrity that is certainly far out of touch with the true sense of the word. For example, in the course content, they attempt to put morality and ethics in one bucket while putting integrity in another bucket. They call it a new model of integrity. The course content creators then make an assumption that their definition of integrity has no rights or wrongs, no values in any absolute sense. They spin their new definition of integrity to suggest that integrity is something that happens in a positive realm only. In other words, for the sake of the model (indoctrination), we must assume that everything goes, everything is relative, and that those who oppose the new definition are thinking and operating in a negative realm.

In a final attempt to divert the students from a true understanding of integrity, they try to simplify the meaning of integrity (their version) as being merely *the act of keeping one's word*. That is it! If you keep your word, you are a person of integrity. I can't make this stuff up! It sounds like relativism to me!

Relativism is "a view that ethical truths depend on the individuals and groups holding them."[6] Relativism is the belief that there is no absolute truth, only the truths that a particular individual or culture happen to believe. If you believe in relativism, then you think different people can have different "true" views about what's moral and immoral. This is an affront to the Bible; therefore, it is an affront to God.

Authenticity: The Secular Humanist definition of authenticity is about being in touch with your inner-self and allowing the natural self-expression of man and his greatness to come shining through, devoid of any spiritual connectivity to the Creator God. They would argue that you can only be authentic when you have voided yourself of any type of worldview or what they would call a *functional constraint*. In other words, if you are holding on to any preconceived worldview (e.g. a Christian worldview), you are not being wholly authentic. You would be considered broken. This form of leadership encourages a re-wiring and/or breakdown of any preconceived notions. Then and only then can true authenticity can be realized. This is brainwashing at its zenith!

Bigger than yourself: It is no surprise, then, that Secular Humanists depend on their ingenuity to solve the world's ills. They would argue that "being one with mankind" is the ultimate expression of selflessness. The cause that they support and want to engender is a universal connectivity to man's greatness and goodness while vehemently discarding the doctrine of the Adamic sin nature of man! It's a New-Age approach to be sure.

Although there is great diversity among the beliefs and practices found within the New Age movement, according to York it is united by a shared "vision of radical mystical transformation on both the personal and collective levels." The movement aims to create "a spirituality without borders or confining dogmas" that is inclusive and pluralistic.[7]

Being cause in the matter: For the Secular Humanists, being cause in the matter is nothing more than taking a stand, speaking out, and putting into action their fundamental beliefs that support their core ideology. In some strange way, they believe they can do this by participating in life from a subjective reality that is divorced from the real world. I believe they create this subjective reality to keep their followers at arm's length from the absolute truth of God's Word. When their followers wander back into objective reality, they are forced to deal with the authority of God and His sovereign control. They teach a separation from reality to maintain mind control.

Now that we have exposed the cult-like New-Age approach of the Secular Humanist in our public colleges and universities, what should be our approach to the leaders who are spewing this nonsensical rhetoric and Humanist indoctrination? I recommend bringing it back to the basics of Bible-based truths. Let's bring the conversation back to Christ and emphasize the following principles:

Integrity, morality, and ethics are all intertwined and related.

Finally, brethren, whatsoever things are true, whatsoever things are honest, whatsoever things are just, whatsoever things are pure, whatsoever things are lovely, whatsoever things are of good report; if there be any virtue, and if there be any praise, think on these things. (Phil. 4:8)

There is absolute truth in the Word of God.

> For this cause also thank we God without ceasing, because, when ye received the word of God which ye heard of us, ye received it not as the word of men, but as it is in truth, the word of God, which effectually worketh also in you that believe. (1 Thess. 2:13)

I live for a cause greater than myself, the glorification of my Savior, and not the prominence and glorification of mankind and his knowledge.

> Whether therefore ye eat, or drink, or whatsoever ye do, do all to the glory of God. (1 Cor. 10:31)

Man was born with a sin nature.

> Nevertheless death reigned from Adam to Moses, even over them that had not sinned after the similitude of Adam's transgression, who is the figure of him that was to come. (Rom. 5:14)

Authenticity starts by telling the truth, fully disclosing what the Word of God says about leadership.

> Speaking lies in hypocrisy; having their conscience seared with a hot iron... (1 Tim. 4:2)

> Sanctify them through thy truth: thy word is truth. (John 17:17)

In conclusion, I hope and pray that this chapter has given to you additional insight into how Secular Humanists are twisting Biblical leadership principles. As Christians, it should give us cause for great concern! Through the use of the mirroring techniques, Satan has closely scripted important elements of Christian responsibility and principles in leadership instruction for his own use. Seemingly within close proximity to our own core values, Secular Humanists have attempted to deceive the world and wrest control of the hearts, minds, and souls of Americans.

CHRISTIAN LEADERSHIP WORLDVIEW: PRINCIPLE #10

The best way to demonstrate and highlight Principle #10 is with a verse from Scripture. 2 Timothy 1:13 states, "Hold fast the form of sound words, which thou hast heard of me, in faith and love which is in Christ Jesus." I believe that this is the epitome of Christian leadership!

---

[1] https://en.wikipedia.org/wiki/secular-humanism

[2] https://en.wikipedia.org/wiki/Mirroring_(psychology)

[3] https://papers.ssrn.com/sol3/papers.cfm?abstract_id=2416455.

[4] www.merriam-webster.com/dictionary/integrity

[5] www.merriam-webster.com/dictionary/authentic

[6] www.merriam-webster.com/dictionary/relativism

[7] https://en.wikipedia.org/wiki/New_Age

Part 4

ROYAL PRIESTS OFFER SACRIFICE

11

CULTIVATING FRIENDSHIPS AND LOYALTY

People don't care how much you know until they know how much you care.

—THEODORE ROOSEVELT

While the first three sections of this book helped us to lay the groundwork for our workplace awareness and responsibility, the next four sections can be described as the application of leadership development. In each subsequent section, we are going to explore various ways to implement our God-given leadership directives.

In this first section, we are going to take the position that, once saved, Christians become one with Christ and take on the spiritual role of being "royal priests." As such, royal priests have the duty to offer up spiritual sacrifices.

> Ye also, as lively stones, are built up a spiritual house, a holy priesthood, to offer up spiritual sacrifices, acceptable to God by Jesus Christ. (1 Peter 2:5)

Let's consider some of the primary ways that we can offer up spiritual sacrifices in a workplace context to demonstrate our love for God and other people (co-workers) to bring praise and honor to God's name.

Cultivating loyalties and friendships (unequally yoked) in God's workplace environment is a significant first step in our Christian testimonies. This sends a signal that we are willing to get beyond the confines of self so we can reach out to others with a concern for their needs. We shouldn't reach out in any self-serving or manipulative fashion. We should reach out to get to know them right where they are by finding out who they are (e.g. their interests, family background, hobbies, and the difficulties they face). This will help us to minister to them more effectively.

Theodore Roosevelt had it right in the quote at the top of this chapter. When we apply the same logic to the workplace context, we can expect that our co-workers "will let us in" as they believe that we truly care about them. They want to know that our motives are not cold, calculating, or self-serving.

In addition, our workplace relationships that we build with the opposite sex must be closely guarded. While we do not want to be unequally yoked in any fashion (male or female), we must put on the righteousness of Christ and build workplace loyalty and friendships to further the Kingdom of God.

Outside of Jesus Himself (who is the supreme example), I believe we can look to the Apostle Paul as an excellent example for building loyalty and friendships.

> And the next day we touched at Sidon. And Julius courteously entreated Paul, and gave him liberty to go unto his friends to refresh himself. (Acts 27:3)

In a very short period of time (the next day), Paul was able build the relationships and loyalty necessary to be courteously treated and given liberty. The liberty given to Paul by Julius was no small gesture. Julius was a centurion with enormous responsibility. As a professional in the Roman army, he was someone who had many men under his command. His task to deliver Paul to Rome and to the emperor was of the highest magnitude. The order to deliver Paul put both he and his men's lives at stake. Failure would have surely been met with quick judgment and death. Why then take a chance and let Paul roam free (pun fully intended) with such liberty?

Paul understood the importance of getting involved in the lives of others. He also understood that building loyalty, trust, and friendships were keys to reaching others for the glory of the Lord.

When I think about the life of Paul, several key aspects of his Christianity come to mind.

First, he loved God with all of his heart, mind, soul, and strength.

Second, he knew the necessity of being involved in the lives of other people.

Third, he wanted to authentically care for others through as many mentoring opportunities as he could possibly find. Paul understood that investing in people by being a mentor was powerful and produced extraordinary spiritual results.

Fourth, he realized that the fellowship had to be lasting and ongoing. There would be very little fruit if he was simply getting people saved, checking the box of evangelism, and moving on to the next convert. He desired to stay connected either through letters or face-to-face meetings. Once the ungodly were converted, he knew a plan would be needed for continuous communication and fellowship.

CHRISTIAN LEADERSHIP WORLDVIEW: PRINCIPLE #11

The ability to build relationships in the workplace is a vital ingredient of the sacrifice that we offer to the Lord. We must step outside of ourselves and begin to focus on the cares and concerns of others and their well-being. In today's world of technology, we have no excuse. There are multiple platforms available for us to reach out and build loyalty and friendships. In turn, these online encounters will help us to build the necessary trust for face-to-face witnessing opportunities.

12

BRING YOUR "BEST SELF" TO WORK EVERY DAY

Love is the motive for working; joy is the strength for working.

—ANDREW BONAR

C an you imagine what would happen to a workplace culture in which every employee brought his or her "best self" to work every day? Productivity would skyrocket, human resource departments would be a thing of the past, meeting time would be enjoyable and productive, and the organization's results and brand image would be off the charts!

I realize that our world in the 21st century is so enveloped with a "get-to-the-top" ideology and constrained with personal ambition that it is hard to imagine organizations being driven by anything else. In general, organizations want employees who are aggressive and driven, with a singular focus for results. Many of these organizations don't care how you get there. Their motto is "just show me the money."

What if we could take responsibility for our own personal space at work? Let's say that, from this day forward, we purposed in our hearts to bring our "best selves" to work every single day. Doesn't revival start in the hearts of individuals?

Rejoice evermore. Pray without ceasing. In everything give thanks: for this is the will of God in Christ Jesus concerning you. (1 Thess. 5:16-18)

Let's pretend for a minute that every aspect of our workplace existence was wrapped up with rejoicing, praying, and giving of thanks. Do you think that this mindset could have an impact and make a difference? For now, I am not talking about your boss or your co-workers. I am talking about the change that only you can make. I can hear all the naysayers and "yeah butters" out there right now... "Yeah, but you don't understand my boss. I work in a terrible department. I am suffering Christian persecution. I sit next to a bully." Let me reel you back in for a moment. I am only talking about your personal responsibilities at work.

Bringing your "best self" to work is a decision that you must wrestle with before each workday. It should become part of your overall spiritual duty to die daily to the old man within. Anything less than falling prostrate before God and pleading for His help, direction, and guidance will be met with utter failure. Trying to take this on in the flesh will also be met with cynicism and condemnation from co-workers. Strides will be made when it is evident to our fellow employees that the Spirit of God is leading the way. Let's consider a few ordinary and common-sense things we can do for the glory of the Lord while at work.

LEAVE PERSONAL ISSUES AT HOME.

This is one of the most difficult things to bring under control and do. When we think of the ongoing pressures of family life and the numerous challenges that we contend with each day, it seems easier said than done. Even those who have mastered the responsibility of stewarding the family unit will admit that it is hard work. There are many things that can and do go wrong. There are endless course corrections. We encounter onslaughts of surprises and heartaches that many times bring us to our knees. Yes, we should come to our Heavenly Father every day with solemn and expectant prayer. We need to seek His face daily.

REMAIN FRIENDLY, UPBEAT, AND POSITIVE.

If you want to be a true Christian leader, you must embrace the positive side of life. Great leaders exude hope, joy, and confidence. The Bible tells us in Proverbs 18:24, "A man that hath friends must shew himself friendly: and there is a friend that sticketh closer than a brother." We need to show the vibrancy and light of our Savior. We should be so full of the Spirit of God that it is contagious. Our co-workers should see a contagion that can't be attributed to anything in our natural sin nature but only to Christ. In other words, we should have a countenance and glow that can only come from above.

MINIMIZE NEGATIVITY.

I have been around many believers who have this figured out. It simply amazes me. They have a way of turning even the worst situations into the most elegant spiritual food for the Lord. There is an upside and positive aspect in everything they encounter. They are the types of Christians who are genuine in their quests to avoid negativity. For those of us who suffer with this sin, we should lean on the everlasting arms of Jesus for our renewal and rebirth in this area.

EXUDE A JOY AND A CHRISTIAN CONFIDENCE (NOT SELF-CONFIDENCE) ABOUT LIFE.

Most mature Christians with discernment can distinguish between those who suffer with the disease (sin) of self-confidence and those who rely on the Lord. Those who carry themselves with a Christian confidence are quick to deflect praise and show a deference to other people. They give God the glory for every aspect of their lives with sincere humility. The Bible teaches us how we are to esteem others before ourselves.

Let nothing be done through strife or vainglory; but in lowliness of mind let each esteem other better than themselves. (Phil. 2:3)

Are you willing to bring your best self to work every day so that others can see Christ in you?

Christian Leadership Worldview: Principle #12

Christian leaders who are happy, spiritually healthy, and filled with the joy of the Lord will do more to impact others than those who are focused on themselves and everything that is wrong with the world. The best way to begin is by getting your eyes off of yourself and putting them on the needs of other people.

13

PERSPECTIVE-TAKING

When you show deep empathy toward others, their defensive energy goes down, and positive energy replaces it. That's when you can get more creative in solving problems.

—STEPHEN COVEY

A third way we can offer sacrifice in the workplace as "royal priests" is to walk a mile in the shoes of a co-worker. The ability to see the world through someone else's eyes is a leadership trait that is impossible to measure but that brings an enormous amount of value to each workplace encounter. It allows us to communicate with others and lead them in ways not available to those who simply want to bark orders and dictate terms. It is a style of leadership, interaction, and communication with others that sends subtle messages of caring and concern. It also sends a message that any workplace differences relating to rank, experience, power, and influence can be set aside without harm or prejudice. In other words, the communication ground on which we stand is level. Over my career, I have had the opportunity to witness both styles of leadership communication.

First, there are leaders who want to remain aloof and stay above the fray of the day-to-day busyness and clutter. These leaders stay detached from personal relationship-building activity, do not engage in sincere and honest dialogue to get to know others, and keep all interaction extremely formal with cut-and-dry responses. They don't let down their "emotional guard" even for a minute. This style of leadership is much more of a transaction-oriented approach than a relationship-building approach in creating workplace culture. Unfortunately, this will create an environment in which there is very little loyalty or trust. I can tell you from firsthand experience that this leadership style will greatly elevate the level of frustration and despondency in the organization. It becomes much easier for the work to become routine, demanding, and pressure-filled.

The more appropriate and energizing style of leadership communication and interaction happens when we get to know one another on a more personal level. When we genuinely reach out to others and try to understand their perspectives, we change the workplace dynamic. Sharing things with one another helps to foster a more caring, bonding, and democratic style of leadership in which everyone feels valued and appreciated. It tells our fellow co-workers and those we lead that who they are as individuals is meaningful outside of the workplace environment. It also tells them that we recognize they have a life and other interests outside of work that are vital parts of their individual makeup.

Outside of a pride-filled worldview, why wouldn't we want to get to know others? Why wouldn't we want to express interest in the "goings-on" of our fellow teammates? These are the same teammates on whom we must rely to accomplish various workplace objectives every day. Let's look to the Bible and the Apostle Paul for further instruction on the ability to use perspective-taking for the benefit of others.

> For though I be free from all men, yet have I made myself servant unto all, that I might gain the more. And unto the Jews I became as a Jew, that I might gain the Jews; to them that are under the law, as under the law, that I might gain them that are under the law. (1 Cor. 9:19-20)

How beautiful is this verse? Paul was willing to lay everything aside so he could get to know them right where they were in their various stations of life. He was willing to make himself a servant to others by conforming to their respective worlds. Converting sinners was so important to Paul that he was willing to forgo all earthly status to be able to meet the spiritual needs of others. He was willing to lay down all of his worldly credentials (and the list was long) to lead others into a saving knowledge of Jesus. It didn't matter to him whether the person was a Jew or Gentile.

Let's bring the leadership trait of perspective-taking back to the workplace environment. Are you willing to step out and get to know others on a deep and personal level? Are you willing to be a servant to your co-workers and meet them (lawfully) right where they are in life to win them to Christ? What about treating your fellow believers this way as well?

CHRISTIAN LEADERSHIP WORLDVIEW: PRINCIPLE #13

Perspective-taking is a vital part of building workplace relationships. It sends a message to our teammates that we are willing to engage in more than just small talk. In a sense, we are accepting an invitation to participate in another's world that may not have been open to us before. It allows for deeper insight, understanding, and trust at work.

14

LISTENING LOUDLY

The art of effective listening is essential to clear communication, and clear communication is necessary to management success.

—JAMES CASH PENNEY

In today's culture, listening has become a lost art form. For the most part, people have very little patience for sitting still and listening to what the other person is actually saying. The art and manners of listening go much deeper than simply listening to words. Proper listening means disconnecting from everything or everyone that is not involved in the current conversation, putting the technology down, looking each other in the eyes, and sincerely trying to understand the root of what the other person is saying. I use the word "root" as a way to signify that, sometimes, people don't always verbalize what they are trying to get across. The person you are talking to may decide to go down multiple paths of discussion, never hitting on the main premise or the intended purpose of what they are trying to communicate in the first place. In cases like these, we have our work cut out for us.

In this chapter, we'll explore several critical aspects of effective listening.

PUT THE TECHNOLOGY DOWN

I am not a big believer that technology and conversation should go hand-in-hand. When individuals are engaged in dialogue, technology should never become a part of the interaction. Under no circumstances should people read texts or e-mails while engaged in conversation. It is just plain rude. It sends a terrible message that what the other person is discussing is just not important. What is even more fascinating to me is that the person reading the texts or e-mails will often apologize and then continue reading them anyway. I am always embarrassed for the other person. It may be a generational thing, but there are a lot of people like me who are offended when technology is being utilized during a two-way conversation. Then again, maybe it's only one-way; I can't tell.

At a minimum, the technology user should establish an upfront contract with the other person and ask permission to use the device(s) before the conversation begins. At least, both of the conversational participants (or not) have agreed to the rules of the game.

LOOK PEOPLE IN THE EYES

There is no better way to show your enthusiasm and interest in what others are saying than to look at them directly in the eyes. Good conversational intelligence and listening starts with eye contact. Having your shoulders back and head up, looking directly into the eyes of the other person is the proper way to engage in conversation. No, it doesn't have to be a staring contest as you may want to bounce your eyes and look away from time to time as the conversation progresses, but the idea is to maintain eye contact. It always sends a signal to others that you are interested and listening loudly.

Have you ever been in a conversation in which the other participant never engages in eye contact? It leaves one feeling a little uneasy and always wondering what the other person is hiding.

HAVING AN ENJOYABLE TWO-WAY CONVERSATION

A third aspect of listening loudly relates to engaging in an enjoyable two-way conversation. Think about a time when you were on the receiving end of a conversation that lasted for hours that seemed like days because you hardly participated at all. You didn't participate because you weren't allowed to. This type of conversation leaves one frustrated. Yes, there may be times when you are counseling others while sitting quietly and listening is the right way to go. But on the whole, both parties should participate equally. Be mindful that good listening is caring about what other people have to say and is not a platform to make yourself feel good with nonstop chatter.

AFFIRM AND REAFFIRM

As the conversation unfolds, there should always be intervals in which you are asking questions to make sure you understand what the other person is saying. In other words, verbalize a quick summary followed by a question, confirming what you think you heard. This will send another signal that you're following the person in conversation. It will also allow him or her to clarify points of confusion. Question-asking is a powerful tool associated with proper listening.

BODY LANGUAGE IS IMPORTANT

Listening loudly involves the use of body language in various forms. Our facial expressions, posture, and even our arms can play a big role in the way we listen.

Think about the last conversation you had when the other person leaned back in a chair with his or her arms folded. What message did you receive? Perhaps, the person was sending a message that he or she was not interested in what you had to say.

On the other hand, if a person is sitting upright with his or her hands on the table and leaning a little forward, this sends an entirely different message. Nodding one's head from time to time in agreement is another way to affirm that you're listening loudly.

APPLY YOUR EARS

The last and most important way you can apply good listening skills is through Biblical knowledge and instruction. Paying attention and listening to the wisdom found in God's Word should never be a passive event. We are told to apply both our hearts and our ears.

CHRISTIAN LEADERSHIP WORLDVIEW: PRINCIPLE #14

Listening loudly is a way for Christians to offer sacrifice in the workplace. It is another fruitful exercise that takes the focus off of ourselves and puts it squarely on the needs of others. Genuine and authentic listening forces one to be focused on and concerned with what other people are saying. For those who struggle with listening, it is an exercise in humility that will stretch your capacity to demonstrate an important aspect of leadership!

> *Apply thine heart unto instruction, and thine ears to the words of knowledge.*
>
> —PROVERBS 23:12

15

CREATE WINS FOR EVERYONE

*Individual commitment to a group effort… that is what
makes a team work, a company work, a society work, a civili-
zation work.*

—VINCE LOMBARDI

In this chapter, we'll concentrate on the Christian leader's responsibility to recognize, highlight, and augment employees' gifts and
talents in a way that cultivates unity in the workplace. Previously,
we discussed how both spiritual gifts and natural talents should be used
to glorify God. When everyone is using and exercising their talents and
gifts at 100% capacity, the Church flourishes and is blessed. While spiritual gifts are manifested and given to us by God for the edification of
the Church, I believe there can be some carryover of those illuminated
gifts to impact the workplace environment. How do we get diverse
workplace employees "firing on all cylinders" for the good of the organization?

> Now there are diversities of gifts, but the same Spirit. (1
> Cor. 12:4)

Great leaders have the ability to "tease out" and "coach up" the best
that people have to offer. They have the instincts to find and push all
the right buttons for maximum performance. They also have the ability
to paint a picture of hope, success, and victory. When they do, this creates a winning atmosphere for everyone involved. Leaders create wins

when they can get their followers to participate fully with their unique strengths, commit to the team's success, feel valued, and are rewarded and recognized for exceptional individual and team performance.

People in the workplace want to contribute in ways that are meaningful and significant. They want to use their strengths to make an impact on the organizations in which they work. Simply put, employees want to feel valued, and they want to win. When leaders create an environment where everyone is fully participating with their strengths (creating wins) and giving their all, the corresponding teamwork, harmony, and results will quickly follow. Let me give you a real-life example.

Coach Jim Graffam was a 27-year-old men's basketball coach who was awarded his first head coaching job at Bonny Eagle High School in Standish, Maine. As a former outstanding athlete himself, he loved everything about sports. He thrived when he was practicing, competing, and winning. Coach Graffam had the charisma, intelligence, people skills, intensity, and knowledge of the game like no other coach I had ever met before. While he related well to his players, he also expected more from us than we thought we were capable of.

He came to our basketball team during my junior year of high school in 1978. Before Coach Graffam's arrival, we finished with a dismal record and ended up close to last place. For many years prior, Bonny Eagle High School men's basketball teams were considered the doormat of the league. Enter Coach Graffam. Coach was quick to assess the skills and talents of each member on the team. He was a master at putting the players in the right spots for maximum efficiency on the court. He understood that the gifts and talents of each individual were important to the overall goal of winning. Yes, Coach Graffam knew the role that each of the 12 players on the team would play and how to get the best out of us. His coaching strategy was to accentuate the dominant skill set of each of his players and then mold them into complimentary partners on a tightly knit team. That is exactly what he did.

During my junior year, we finished with a winning record. We established a reputation in the Southern-Maine area as a high-energy team that could compete with the best teams around. We weren't yet at an elite level, but every time we went out on the court, we left everything we had on the floor. We caught Coach Graffam's vision and were obsessed with competing and winning!

By the time my senior year rolled around, we all knew that Coach (and we) had created something special. Over the summer, we had all committed to being the best players possible. Many of us attended multiple basketball camps and practiced every day. We spent hundreds of hours shooting baskets and honing our defensive skills. It was during this timeframe that we all began to realize that each of us had a specific role to play. Coach Graffam also let us know in no uncertain terms what he expected from each one of us. All of this led to an incredible playoff run in 1979 that will be a fond memory for the rest of my life.

As 1979 rolled around, we were one of the largest high schools in the state and participated in Class A, which was the top sports league. We finished with 18 wins my senior year and were ranked fifth in the entire state. We made the playoffs for the first time in over a decade and eventually lost to a perennial powerhouse, Rumford. We had left our mark on the basketball landscape in the state of Maine. But how did we accomplish this?

I believe that everyone on the basketball team came to realize we had an enormous responsibility to use our gifts and talents for the betterment of the team and for the good of other people. We all had a role to play, and when we collectively gave it our all, we were able to create something unique and special. This dynamic only took place when Coach Graffam started creating wins for everyone. He focused on and magnified our strengths, established high expectations for success, minimized our deficiencies, and coached us toward a better version of our basketball selves for team success. Sound familiar?

In 2012, Coach Graffam was inducted into the New England Basketball Hall of Fame.

CHRISTIAN LEADERSHIP WORLDVIEW: PRINCIPLE #15

As Christian leaders, we need to be mindful of the unique gifts and talents of others and then utilize those gifts in a way that brings glory to the Lord. Prodding, encouraging, and using tough love are all tools that are at the leader's disposal. Regardless of how one goes about "coaching up" or finding the right buttons to push, leaders strive to get maximum effort from a diverse group of workplace talent. Whether in the ministry, private, or public sectors, the end game is for your followers to be "firing on all cylinders" for the glory of the Lord!

16

Seek the Opinions of Others

Without counsel purposes are disappointed: but in the multitude of counselors they are established.

—Proverbs 15:22

One of the most powerful things a Christian leader can do in the workplace is to ask someone for his or her opinion. Asking a co-worker to weigh in on a subject sounds like a fairly simple and straightforward aspect of leading people; doesn't it? Unfortunately, the question-asking technique often gets lost in the heat of workplace battles. We can get so focused on "getting it right" with the projects that we're working on and making sure the boss is happy that we often overpower our employees, followers, or co-workers with what we think is the best course of action. We let our experience, tenure, title, and pride interfere with one of the most basic tenets of management and human relations. Seeking the opinions of others is another way we can offer sacrifice in the workplace. It shows humility, deference to others, team-building, and much more.

In this chapter, we'll explore the effects of diligently and systematically seeking the opinions of other people while at work. In doing so, we substantiate the wisdom and relevance of God's Word found in the book of *Proverbs*.

> Where no counsel is, the people fall: but in the multitude of counselors there is safety. (Prov. 11:14)

BRINGS DECISION-MAKING CONTEXT

What better way to fill in the gaps of workplace knowledge and decision-making than to seek the opinions and counsel of others. Each one of us has a unique road that God has mapped out for us here on Earth. Our experiences in life, intellectual capacity, family background, job rotations, and reading habits all give us varied perspectives and context. While all believers should have a Biblical worldview, the ways we experience culture, make decisions, and live out our faith are not exact carbon-copies of one another. God is molding us into His image with different trials, tribulations, and life experiences. That is precisely the beauty and wisdom of seeking the opinion of others. Diversity of thought will help to frame the context needed to make sound decisions at work. Leaders of healthy organizations want to end up with the best decisions possible. Purposes will be established (see Prov. 15:22) when you seek the opinions and counsel of others. By doing this, you will foster the democratization of decision-making and flatten the organizational hierarchy while making quicker and more-informed decisions.

BUILDS CONFIDENCE

Anyone who has been on the receiving end of a genuine request for counsel in the workplace will undoubtedly agree that it helps build confidence. As I think back to my corporate experiences, when executives would ask my opinion, I was honored for the opportunity to contribute. While rigorous debate would often ensue before a final decision was rendered, these opportunities helped to build my confidence and to establish credibility.

SUPPLIES RECOGNITION AND REWARD

Picture any workplace scenario where an employee is in a meeting with a group of his or her peers. The boss asks for their specific opinion and counsel on a topic. Perhaps, the boss may even have led into the question by acknowledging the employee's level of expertise and competence in a certain area of business. How would that make you feel? This makes one feel appreciated and valued.

Recognition and reward can take many forms beyond the monetary aspect of why we come to work every day. Earnestly seeking the opinion of others will create one of the highest forms of recognition available in the workplace.

Elevates knowledge base

Inherent in the verse listed above is an understanding that discussion, debate, and logical (Bible-based) sequences of thought will be taken and analyzed. Thoughtful consideration for various alternative courses of action will be evaluated. When one has multiple people counseling him or her, there will be differences of opinion that can help the person to learn and grow. Everyone wins when there is diversity of opinion and thought.

Builds teamwork

Question-asking is an integral part of team-building. Asking for and expecting workplace contribution helps others to feel like valued parts of the team. When each team member is asked to share his or her insight and knowledge on a particular issue of business, this helps with building the cohesiveness needed for maximum efficiency. In the long-term, that cohesiveness leads to trust and the teamwork necessary to get things done.

Produces better results

When leaders seek the opinions of others, results improve. The old saying, "Two heads are better than one," certainly applies. Going alone is never the right thing to do. Seeking diverse counsel, context, expertise, and insight will put one in a position to make good decisions. When we string together enough good decisions, good results will follow.

CHRISTIAN LEADERSHIP WORLDVIEW: PRINCIPLE #16

Christ uses mankind to build His Church. He gives each of us who know Him as Savior a common vision to seek Him and praise His name. He designed a way forward that uses the collective strengths of diverse human beings. This is the same approach that leaders in the workplace need to use. When we seek the opinions of others, we break down the walls of isolation so everyone can contribute.

17

BE FULLY PRESENT

Concentrate all your thoughts upon the work at hand. The sun's rays do not burn until brought to a focus.

—ALEXANDER GRAHAM BELL

The culture in which we live has produced unparalleled emphasis on scurrying around in a frantic-like fashion, checking all of the boxes on our daily "to do" lists. Many of us have decided to put our track shoes on and have determined to win the activities race in which there is no room left for connections with other people. The intensity of life has reached such a fever pitch that the motto "take time to smell the roses" seems almost laughable. Yet, we continue to pride ourselves on our ability to multitask and cram as many things as possible into a 24-hour period.

When was the last time you recalibrated your schedule or decided to slow things down a little to avoid missing out on important interactions and conversations? How can we wade through all of the cultural noise and complexity out there so we can boil things down to a handful of heavenly priorities? As we wade through the noise and complexity, are we giving people our undivided attention? It seems as though one's ability to be fully present for the good of others has come to a grinding halt.

When Christ initiated His public ministry, He was a relatively unknown rabbi to most of the people in the region. He was a 30-year-old carpenter from Nazareth who began drawing the attention of locals with stories (parables) that captivated the imagination of their hearts. It wasn't too long before the power, wisdom, and authority with which He spoke elevated Him to increasing levels of notoriety. He soon began performing miracles and healing all manner of disease and sickness. His power appeared to know no limits or bounds. He had the power to overcome nature, death, the spiritual world, disease, sickness, and every other physical and spiritual manifestation known to man. Everywhere He went, throngs of people vied to get a glimpse of this unlikely human phenomenon. But even in the midst of the endless number of people trying to get His attention, Christ had the ability to focus on immediate and important spiritual matters. He had the ability to be *fully present* and to see the needs of others. This is a gift that has certainly eluded many of us and is more difficult to come by in the 21st century.

> And, behold, a woman, which was diseased with an issue of blood twelve years, came behind him, and touched the hem of his garment: For she said within herself, If I may but touch his garment, I shall be whole. *But Jesus turned him about*, and when he saw her, he said, Daughter, be of good comfort; thy faith hath made thee whole. And the woman was made whole from that hour. (Matt. 9:20-22)

While the distractions were many, Jesus turned around and considered the needs of the woman. What a perfect picture we have of Jesus cutting through the activity and busyness of the hour to turn and give His undivided attention to this woman. He could have spent time with the Pharisees, ruling elite, lawyers, and other influential people of the day, but Christ chose to turn and spend time with a woman who needed His help. He was fully aware of this woman's need (issue of blood) and was compassionate enough to do something about it. Jesus was and is always conscious of the lowly, poor, needy, and downtrodden. Christ knows the difference between the busyness and activity of life and moments of true importance.

Christ's example is one that leaders should be using in the workplace. How many times have business leaders or others in positions of authority walked right past those who are less fortunate, lower down in the organizational hierarchy, or have different career aspirations and goals than their own? Think of the positive impact of stopping, shaking an employee's hand, and being fully present for just a few moments. Those who are engaged in this type of behavior will leave a lasting impression on others.

When I was a young and impressionable sales employee in my mid-20s, I had recently been promoted to my first sales position and was attending a district meeting in Boston, Massachusetts. After three and a half years of working in operations, I had my first opportunity to get to the next level of the company. The entire district operations and sales teams were asked to attend the annual kick-off meeting. This was a big deal for me and was my first chance to meet my counterparts in New England. We were all staying at one of the well-known elite hotels in downtown Boston. I remember thinking that I had finally "arrived" and was feeling pretty good about myself.

While in the area, I figured I would get together with a close college friend who lived nearby. At the end of the first day of our meeting, we adjourned around 5 p.m., so my college buddy and I made plans to meet in the lobby at 6 p.m. sharp. Everything worked according to plan, and we decided to walk around town and stop for dinner. As my friend and I were leaving the hotel, I noticed that several of the key district personnel (district manager, district sales manager, labor manager, and district engineer) were headed my way. As they reached the area where my college friend and I were standing, they kept walking and headed out the door. My bosses, who knew I was someone who had just been promoted, made a decision not to acknowledge a lowly sales representative. I was embarrassed and crushed all at the same time. Now 35 years later, I can still recount with vivid detail the events of that night. The Lord was showing me something about leadership as well as my pride, and He wanted me to remember this situation for the future.

At another point in my career, I was asked to run a trucking facility in Camden, New Jersey. It was an opportunity to run a very large facility with hundreds of employees. While I wasn't too happy about moving to New Jersey, I was excited to see that all of my hard work in Colchester, Vermont was paying off. They offered me an additional $100 per week and asked me to think about it and get back to them. During the next two weeks, my wife and I began checking out the cost of living expenses and realized that anything short of an additional $300 per week wouldn't work. Even then, we would be cutting the family budget pretty close. I called my immediate boss, the district manager, and told him of my predicament. He went ballistic on the phone and wasn't happy with me. He told me my career was "dead in the water."

Once again, the Lord took this opportunity to teach me something about true leadership. A few months later, we had a district meeting, and the regional vice president who had recommended me for the promotion was in attendance. There were close to a thousand people at this meeting. At the end of the meeting, the regional vice president spoke to our group and then headed out the door. I caught his attention, and he allowed himself to be *fully present* with me. Even as hundreds of other employees walked by, his eyes locked onto mine as he gave his full and uninterrupted attention to me. I knew right then what it meant to be fully present. This VP demonstrated a courtesy to me that is still with me 35 years later. (By the way, that VP went on to become the CEO of the company. That didn't surprise me.)

CHRISTIAN LEADERSHIP WORLDVIEW: PRINCIPLE #17

There is something significant and heartwarming when an individual decides to give to you his or her full and undivided attention by being fully present. No distractions, phone calls, texts, e-mails, or other interruptions. One gets the sense that the other person actually cares. It is a courtesy that we would all do well to heed and implement into our relationship-building activities. Are you fully present for others?

18

EXUDE SIMPLICITY IN CONVERSATION

Truth is ever to be found in simplicity, and not in the multiplicity and confusion of things.

—ISAAC NEWTON

Royal priests can offer sacrifice in the workplace by relating well to people in conversation. There's a reason why some people rise to the top of organizational charts while others don't. Hard work, experience, knowledge, conviction for a cause, results, and the ability to communicate well all play large roles in leading. In this chapter, we'll explore the substance and style of how one goes about leading through communication.

There isn't any doubt that one needs to have the intellectual capacity, experience, and job knowledge to be a truly effective leader in the workplace. Leaders must possess the depth and breadth of industry and organizational knowledge to establish credibility. Employees look to their leaders to be able to quickly assess volatile business situations and make key decisions while setting the strategic agenda for the future. Having a novice in a key position of leadership is a formula for disaster.

Please don't misunderstand the reasoning here. There are certainly different levels of leadership decision-making ability and business acuity needed in all parts of an organization. That is how employees gain the incremental knowledge and experience needed to take on additional responsibility. Leaders need to prove that they can handle (with results) a specific job function or project before getting promoted to the next level.

At least, this is how it should work and does work in most areas of employment (nepotism excluded).

When I was a baseball player, I experienced this incremental approach to responsibility. When I signed a professional baseball contract with the Montreal Expos, they assigned me to Class A (Low A) out in Calgary, Alberta, Canada. This was just one stop along the road of the many potential levels of professional baseball in the organization. Class A (Low A), Class A (High A), Class AA (Double A), and Class AAA (Triple A) were the stepping stones to reach the major leagues. Each stop prepares baseball players to play a higher and more experienced level of baseball. Each stop also allows the players to hone their skills and to experiment with different styles of play until they become ready to produce the necessary results.

For the most part, it is the same way in business. Yes, there are some highly talented employees out there who may be able to move at a faster pace, but the reality is they are expected to have the experience and knowledge necessary to perform at high levels.

However, possessing all of the knowledge and experience is just the starting point for being a successful leader. Knowledge and experience will get one nowhere if one lacks the ability to communicate in a manner that ingratiates oneself to others.

We all can relate to those who we might put into the "nutty professor" category. This type of employee is incredibly gifted in his or her respective areas of expertise but are so intelligent in certain areas that they can't communicate and lead others. They have the inability to relate and communicate with others at their level. Granted, there are some who have both the intellect and the ability to communicate effectively. Those are the leaders who will rise to the top. But this is a rare combination in the workplace environment. Many aspiring leaders are either dispossessed of the experience and knowledge needed, or they struggle to verbalize a clear vision for where they want to go and how they want to get there.

Great leaders also need to be able to take complex issues (knowledge and experience) and craft the messaging (communication) in a way that it can be understood at all levels of the organization. They know how to synthesize complex information and then relate key business themes in a style that exudes simplicity. True servant leaders have no need to elevate their self-worth through a grandiose and self-aggrandizing style of leadership with words people can't understand. Employees are not interested in some intellectual diatribe of issues that don't apply to them. Great leaders have the ability to understand what people want and then cut to the chase in simple terms so that everyone can easily understand the issues at hand. The Word of God has a lot to say about the style of leadership communication needed, and it has broad application in the workplace.

> For our rejoicing is this, the testimony of our conscience, that in *simplicity and godly sincerity*, not in fleshly wisdom, but by the grace of God, we have had our conversation in the world, and more abundantly to you-ward. (2 Cor. 1:12)

This verse does an outstanding job of stripping away any form of man-made wisdom or intellectualism that may exist among leaders. We must never let intellectualism corrupt our way of thinking and how we communicate with those we lead. Intellectualism and fleshly wisdom scream of a prideful and selfish inner core. Each has the potential danger of leading to a "me"-focused versus a God-focused style of communication. I believe that intellectualism and pride are two sides of the same coin. God tells us throughout Scripture that He wants us to imitate His Son. As image-bearers for the glory of the Lord, we need to communicate in a style that emulates our Savior. Jesus is the Master at communicating in broad and simple terms that give us hope for a better tomorrow.

CHRISTIAN LEADERSHIP WORLDVIEW: PRINCIPLE #18

Let's never forget the model of communication given to us in the Bible. Even as we grow in our positions of workplace responsibility and leadership, let's remember that simplicity and godly sincerity are the best leadership communication styles available. While the complexity of workplace issues is great, and the knowledge and understanding needed to solve them are equal, we need to communicate with one another on equal terms. We must exude simplicity in our conversation for the glory of the Lord!

19

STAY POSITIVE

Positive thinking will let you do everything better than negative thinking will.

—ZIG ZIGLAR

Crisis environments at work will test the moral character, strength of conviction, and resolve of workplace leadership. When the pressures at work start mounting with waves that seem like they are 30-feet high, causing seemingly insurmountable conditions, the true test of leadership will be actualized. How do you respond (lead) at work in crisis situations or in conditions that present themselves as unwelcome surprises? Do you operate in the flesh or go to the Savior, looking for the peace that passes all understanding (Phil. 4:7)? When we stay positive through crisis situations, this is another way to offer sacrifice unto the Lord.

Followers want to see their leaders lead in a manner that demonstrates an even-tempered and positive response in face of difficulty and marketplace pressures. They don't want leaders who are tossed to and fro with every wind of organizational change. No, employees want consistency from those who lead them. They want to know that their leaders will do and say all the right things, even in the face of adversity. While the pessimist will point to 1,001 reasons for all that is wrong with an organization in crisis, the true leader steps up and looks for ways to solve "challenges" for the good of the organization and for others. Christian leaders should cherish moments of truth during crisis situations as these will help to define their Christian testimonies and separate them from worldly thinking and decision-making. Isn't that what we are trying to do in the first place? Don't we want people at work to see Christ in us? Don't we want them to see a big difference in the way that we work through crises?

Employees in the workplace want to see their leaders demonstrate an optimistic and enthusiastic attitude when the chips are down. In crisis environments, they want to hear their leaders say, "We will get through this. It's going to be okay. Here's what we are going to do to solve the problem. Let's jump on this right away and get this done." They want a steady hand in times of turmoil. Leaders need to stay calm, cool, and collected even when the seas start swelling.

When I was a new facility manager in Burlington, Vermont, we brought a large customer on board that went from zero to $1 million in a very short period of time. It had an enormous impact on both our revenue and profits. We went from being considered an "under-water facility" (words of our president) to one that was growing in respectability.

The additional $1 million came with a price, however. It brought an additional degree of operational difficulty for meeting customer needs. The new customer was extremely demanding, and when he wanted something, he expected us to make it happen with no questions asked.

As I look back on the demanding nature of this one customer, I realize that he taught me a lot about leadership in crisis situations. For whatever reason, every time this customer would call, it seemed like "the house was on fire." Well, our new customer had one consistent habit that taught our team about leading in crisis environments. Nearly every Friday afternoon at around 4:45 p.m., our new customer would call with a request. These weren't any run-of-the-mill type of requests, either. He would call wanting us to pull an operational rabbit out of our hat. Trying to meet his demands would turn our operations inside out. Of course, at 5 p.m. on a Friday, our entire team had our eyes on the prize of getting out the door to enjoy the weekend.

What has always stayed with me regarding those many Friday nights when he would call (which usually meant working Saturday), was the way he approached each situation. He would start the conversation by saying, "Michael, I have an opportunity for you." Our new customer framed the crisis situation in a way that changed our mindset and thinking. We now had a positive opportunity to help our customer rather than viewing it merely as a negative situation. In a sense, we had an opportunity to prove our value to him all over again. I can't tell you how many times over the years I used that same phrase.

Christians should find "opportunities" to help in the workplace exciting and exhilarating. If we can keep Psalm 32:11 at the forefront of our minds, everything will come into focus.

> Be glad in the Lord, and rejoice, ye righteous: and shout
> for joy, all ye that are upright in heart. (Psalm 32:11)

If we are truly glad in the Lord, rejoicing and shouting for joy, how can we meltdown and shrink when faced with difficult circumstances at work?

CHRISTIAN LEADERSHIP WORLDVIEW: PRINCIPLE #19

Marketplace leaders should point to a cause much bigger than any situation or crisis. Christian leaders have a duty to glorify God with positive and upbeat words and actions. When tasked with navigating through difficult workplace situations, go to the Lord in prayer and ask for guidance and direction. When you get your prayers answered, give the honor and praise to Him!

20

STRENGTHEN OTHERS

A life is not important except in the impact it has on other lives.

—JACKIE ROBINSON

C hristian marketplace leaders must desire to strengthen their followers spiritually, morally, and intellectually. They should understand the importance of winning the battle in the workplace for the hearts, minds, and souls of their fellow employees. Leaders should see our need to provide for our families as a means to an end rather than an end in itself. In other words, our God-given need to labor for our food, clothing, and shelter so we can take care of our family members should be an extension of our Christian duty and responsibility. It shouldn't be an all-consuming focus on "the work" only. Our Christian duty and responsibility is to strengthen others through soul-building, heart-building, and mind-building training and insights that move others to identify with Christ. The end game is to win others to Christ and build believers up in the faith while at work.

As explained in the introductory chapter of this book, relational, conceptual, and vocational leadership are the foundation of the principles in this book. This chapter will help to expound upon those key principles. In this section of the book, we have explained that *offering sacrifice* means a focus and concern for other people. Strengthening others is the epitome of that sacred call-to-action in the workplace.

Iron sharpeneth iron; so a man sharpeneth the countenance of his friend. (Prov. 27:17)

STRENGTHENS OTHERS SPIRITUALLY

Christians should pray every day that they will be given specific opportunities at work to proclaim the name of Jesus so that others will come to a saving knowledge of Him. How are you doing? Do you have a list of nonbelievers for whom you are praying? Are they at the top of your mind each day as you go to work? Are you asking God to intervene in the workplace and open up avenues for witnessing? The challenge and difficulty to do so in the 21st century is certainly formidable; however, this doesn't negate our duty to proclaim Jesus.

Each day, Christian leaders must be on the lookout for witnessing opportunities. I have spent 33 years in the business world, and I can tell you without hesitation that the opportunities to verbalize Christ are endless. He will provide the exact conditions in His good timing. When we have our spiritual radars of discernment fine-tuned through His Word, the situations will present themselves.

What about fellow believers in the faith? Christian leaders should be willing to reach out to those believers who are not as mature in the faith and help them reach new levels of spiritual maturity and growth. The same thought process and logic for strengthening others spiritually applies to Christian believers as well.

At one of my previous places of employment, we had just finished putting together a mentoring program that was the first of its kind at the company I was working with at the time. We had hundreds of interested employees who wanted to participate in the mentoring program. Of course, we needed both mentors and mentees to make the program work. I opted to be a mentor for the duration of the program. I had more than 30 years of business experience and hoped I could be a blessing both vocationally and spiritually. God blew the doors wide-open for me to mentor two young believers in the faith.

At the time, God convicted me to put together a mentoring and training program at work, which eventually became the foundation of the Christian training material I use around the globe today. We went through an abbreviated and synthesized eight-week version of much of the material in this book. It is fascinating to me to see what God can do when we are willing to be used for His glory. I had no idea where the Lord would be taking me, but He knew. Even when you work for organizations that are driven by Secular Humanist philosophies and governance that are anti-God, He will open up witnessing and edifying opportunities if you are willing. Praise God!

STRENGTHENS OTHERS MORALLY

Our existence here on Earth is to imitate and not to create. I believe that the Lord designed it this way because of His intimate knowledge of the dregs of human nature. God knows that, when man is focused on creating something new, exciting, and revolutionary, man will often lay claim and take all of the credit.

On the other hand, when we imitate our Lord and Savior and His divine moral character, we have no option but to give Him all of the honor and glory. The Lord is saying to us, "Because I created you and know the old man within and his wretched tendencies, here is how I am going to go about creating you in My image." He uses the progressive-sanctification process based solely on imitation. Yes, that is one of our primary responsibilities while at work. We are directed to put on the mind of Christ and not to serve the law of sin with our fleshly and carnal thinking.

> I thank God through Jesus Christ our Lord. So then with the mind I myself serve the law of God; but with the flesh the law of sin. (Rom. 7:25)

God has preserved His moral law in the context and boundaries of His Word, and we see His divine moral attributes throughout Scripture. In fact, He tells us that His moral law is written on our hearts.

For not the hearers of the law are just before God, but the doers of the law shall be justified. For when the Gentiles, which have not the law, do by nature the things contained in the law, these, having not the law, are a law unto themselves: Which shew the work of the law written in their hearts, their conscience also bearing witness, and their thoughts the mean while accusing or else excusing one another. (Rom. 2:13-15)

In the workplace, we are to make decisions and conduct ourselves in ways that imitate His love, joy, peace, long-suffering, gentleness, goodness, faith, meekness, temperance, mercy, grace, justice, righteousness, holiness, and truth. When we do so, we strengthen others morally. We help them comply with the precepts and conditions of what absolute truth actually looks like. Therefore, we help our co-workers imitate an entirely different standard of morality and ethics, one that is aligned with His Word.

STRENGTHENS OTHERS INTELLECTUALLY

Strengthening and sharpening our co-workers means that we will greatly impact and challenge the minds and intellectual capacity of others. Whether it is to help train others in a specific aspect of work-related processes, industry knowledge, business acumen, or critical thinking, strengthening the mind is crucial to our leadership credentials. Ultimately, we want the people with whom we interact at work to form a *Christian leadership worldview*. While the totality of this worldview will not be accepted in most organizations, we want to leave our Christian "markers" on others (in as many ways as possible) for the glory of God through each decision, communication, and interaction we are involved with while at work. We want all of our co-workers to acknowledge that our approach to "thinking" about issues is unique and uncommon (in a good way). We want them to realize that our way of contemplating and thinking through workplace issues comes from a radically different space (a spiritual one) from the rest of the world. We want them to see the vitality, sincerity, authenticity, integrity, and absolute truth of our way of thinking about issues. In the end, we want our co-workers to desire to have the same worldview. This worldview begins and ends with the foundational truths found in His Word.

CHRISTIAN LEADERSHIP WORLDVIEW: PRINCIPLE #20

Christian leaders must determine to strengthen others on purpose while at work. We must diligently and thoughtfully consider how we are going to strengthen others spiritually, morally, and intellectually. Leadership like this doesn't just happen. It is derived from a commitment, drive, and determination (like no other) to live out our faith in the workplace domain. In many respects, this is a spiritual domain that we need to recapture for the Lord.

Part 5

Royal Priests Proclaim

21

USE GOOD JUDGEMENT

There is no responsibility in the marketplace that can approach the enormity of proclaiming Christ and the essence of the glory of God.

As royal priests (Christians) in the workplace, we have a responsibility to *proclaim* the Savior in how we carry out the particular functions of leadership. There are at least 10 specific ways we can shout out the name of the Lord through our conduct that acknowledge Christian distinctiveness. We must take the focus away from "self" (dying to self) and focus on the development of others. We offer sacrifice to the Lord by building others up with a loving and selfless approach to the workplace.

Leadership also involves developing high-quality and disciplined personal standards of excellence that help to frame our individual Christian brands (testimonies). The ways we carry out our workplace responsibilities (micro-components of leadership) will build life-long stories of the leaders we aspire to become (macro-components of leadership). There is an amalgamation and cascading impact of the various components of leadership that speak to who we have become (or are perceived to be) at work. We need to be showing forth the praises of Him who called us out of darkness!

> But ye are a chosen generation, a royal priesthood, a holy nation, a peculiar people; that ye should show forth the praises of him who hath called you out of darkness into his marvelous light. (1 Pet. 2:9)

The first way we can show forth the praises of Him who called us out of darkness is to use good judgment with discerning wisdom. First, we must separate the world's "no-holds-barred" approach to getting organizational results at any and all costs from the strategy and tactics that reflect the patience, thoughtfulness, and counsel needed to render meaningful judgment with discerning wisdom. The book of *Proverbs* can shed much light on the patience needed for skilled living. Judgment with discerning wisdom should be slow to materialize.

> The thoughts of the diligent tend only to plenteousness;
> but of every one that is hasty only to want. (Prov. 21:5)

> Seest thou a man that is hasty in his words? there is more
> hope of a fool than of him. (Proverbs 29:20)

Using good judgment with discerning wisdom requires calculated and contemplative approaches. The hasty in spirit and in words will suffer the consequences of rash and untimely behavior and decision-making while at work. Generally speaking, there is nothing good that can come from our rash and spur-of-the-moment actions. Unfortunately, it puts us in a box where the results of our actions are difficult to reverse. These actions will not go unnoticed by those in authority over us.

Next, we must make sure that the filter of God's Word is the last and ultimate authority in our judgment. We should compare all of our workplace decisions with the wisdom found in His Word. Does this sound a little over-the-top to you? It shouldn't. You would be surprised how those in the workforce can manipulate and reframe absolute truth and moral values in ways that are contrary to His Word. When you start down the path of making all of your workplace decisions in the flesh (outside of absolute truth found in the Bible), it is just a matter of time before it comes back to bite you. When it does, your Christian reputation is stained forever. It is next to impossible to "walk back" major decisions that go sideways. There are some bosses who will look for someone to blame and try to lay the entanglement at the feet of someone else.

What does wisdom look like in the workplace? Is there a difference from any other display of Biblical wisdom? The short answer is... *no*, there is not. While the workplace presents a unique spiritual domain in which we must learn to operate with various degrees of complexity, the godly wisdom needed at work is the same wisdom found in the book of *James* in the Bible.

> But the wisdom that is from above is first pure, then peaceable, gentle, and easy to be entreated, full of mercy and good fruits, without partiality, and without hypocrisy. (Jas. 3:17)

Would we even need a human resources department if the pure and unadulterated spirit mentioned in this verse was lived out in the workplace? I think not!

CHRISTIAN LEADERSHIP WORLDVIEW: PRINCIPLE #21

Patience, wise counsel, and the filter of God's Word will give you the moral authority to make decisions that are full of good judgment with discerning wisdom.

22

RELATIONSHIPS VS. TRANSACTIONS

Leaders understand the ultimate power of relationships.

—TOM PETERS

Over the last three decades, businesses across the globe have greatly benefited from the explosion of technology advances. The progress that has been made with technology is nothing less than astounding! It seems like, every day, a revolutionary new technology product is being released or an upgrade to an existing technology is emerging. It has changed our society, culture, and our way of doing business and relating to others. Technology has also brought an extremely high degree of automation that allow the companies we work for to streamline operations, reduce overall costs, and bring a level of quality never before seen in the marketplace. Even Ford Motors, who was way out in front with innovative technology, having introduced the moving assembly line, continues to make extraordinary technology strides.

> As today marks the 100th anniversary of the moving assembly line invented by Ford Motor Company under the leadership of Henry Ford, the company is building on its legacy of innovation by expanding advanced manufacturing capabilities and introducing groundbreaking technologies that could revolutionize mass production for decades to come.[1]

There is no doubt that we have all benefited from the impact that automation has provided through technology advances. Specialization through automation has had the effect of systematizing processes and raising the level of quality standards while improving cost-control and efficiency. However, beyond the intricacies of highly engineered robotics, the sophistication of integrated systems, and an automation approach to the marketplace, technology has also greatly changed the ways in which we interact and communicate, both professionally and personally.

A few months ago, I was at the grocery store waiting in a long line at the checkout counter, hoping to get some quick service. While I was there, I started observing the various styles of the two attendants who were checking us out. The first was a young lady in her late 20s who seemed to be very efficient. She asked the same business-related questions, used the same short-and-stiff business type of greetings, and seemed to be moving people through the line at a fairly reasonable pace. She never went off script and never once looked up to make eye contact with those she was serving. As transactions go, it was efficient. But from a customer's perspective, the experience was sterile and without any real care or concern for who I am. I thought to myself that she was an outstanding human automaton, diligently providing meaningless transactions to the hundreds of people she was ushering out the door.

Then, I looked across the aisle to observe how the other checkout attendant was performing her job responsibilities. This woman was in her mid-40s and seemed to have a joyful countenance and happy way of expressing herself to the customers. She, too, appeared to have the line moving along at a pretty good clip but offered much more than a simple transaction. During the checkout process, she always took the time to get to know the customers with whom she was interacting. On several occasions, she waited on people she already knew. It was obvious that this employee worked hard at building relationships with the people she served.

That encounter at the grocery store caused me to think about technology in general and its overall impact in the workplace. Specifically, has technology dumbed-down our ability to communicate with and care for our co-workers (neighbors)?

One of the unfortunate carryovers from the technology revolution is that every work process, exchange, and interaction is so tightly scripted and automated that there isn't much room left for relationship-building. *Transactions* make us feel good. We can go to the boss and talk about productivity increases and the sheer number of customers with whom we have transacted during the workday. We can go to our e-mails, texts, and the social media platforms that technology has afforded us and carry on conversations from afar with very little skin in the game. In other words, we can interact with an endless number of factoids that do very little to build up other people in the faith.

There are many in society who willingly use technology as a shield and protectant against social awkwardness. Others have grown up in a highly saturated technology environment and don't fully realize that their relationship-building skills have been diminished or impaired. *Relationships*, on the other hand, take a lot more of our time and require hard work.

What I saw that day in the grocery store was a tale of two relationship-building worldviews related to the care and concern for others. One was determined to build relationships for the long-term, impacting lives. The other was just trying to get people through the line as quickly as possible.

I know what you are thinking. You are thinking that, if you are at a grocery store, you may want to get out of the store as fast as possible, too. However, beyond the grocery store lines, let's think about the broader implications for society at large. If all we are focused on while at work is just another transaction, what does that say about society as a whole? If we have no desire to build long-lasting relationships with others, what does that say about our Christianity?

Granted, there are those at the top of some organizations who can look at you (or look right through you) as just another transaction, and they seem to be getting along just fine. We have all been around them. It's all business with these types of leaders. It's highly impersonal and requires little to no "soft skills" to interact with others. I don't consider them true leaders.

True Christian leaders look for opportunities to build long-lasting relationships. These are the leaders who have your best interests at heart. They want to take the time to get to know you on a personal level with a concern and respect for you as an individual. It's almost hard to imagine them operating in any other way. Their whole essence of being and interacting with the world is geared toward relationships. The best way to describe it is to say that true Christian leaders get their vibrancy and "fuel" from interacting with and impacting the lives of others.

Remember that we are not numbers (transactions) but human beings with real feelings, concerns, and needs. Christian leaders need to show others that they really care.

How are you doing on the relationship-building front at your place of employment? Are you interacting through transactions or relationships? Does technology impede or improve your ability to develop close and long-lasting relationships for the glory of God?

CHRISTIAN LEADERSHIP WORLDVIEW: PRINCIPLE #22

Christian leaders must be discerning enough to know that technology has the potential to push others into a "transaction mindset" where vital relationships are being managed remotely. Developing true commitment, trusted friendships, and honest communication can be set aside with the push of a button. We need relationships (kindly affection)... not transactions!

> Be kindly affectioned one to another with brotherly love; in honor preferring one another.
>
> —ROMANS 12:10

---

[1] www.corporate.ford.com/innovation/100-years-moving-assembly-line.html

23

ALLOW VULNERABILITY

Vulnerability is about showing up and being seen. It's tough to do that when we're terrified about what people might see or think.

—BRENE BROWN

The contents of this chapter will certainly fly in the face of the world's version of leadership. The stereotypical leaders of today are depicted as men and women who never flinch or show any kind of emotion, have a stiff upper lip, and are hard-charging right to the very end. One may even refer to them as the "Teflon Dons" of leadership who nothing seems to impact on any emotional level. This stereotype depicts them as tough, demanding, unwavering, and sometimes mean to the core. Anything less and they are considered weak and not fit to lead.

Does that sound like the type of Christian leader that you want to be in the workplace?

Let's now compare the world's version of leadership to what I call the "gold standard" of leading others. There are two verses that I believe speak directly to the concept of *allowing vulnerability*, which is the central point of this chapter.

Jesus wept. (John 11:35)

How beautiful and appropriate are those two words found in the shortest verse of the Bible? Jesus wept. Here, we have the Creator of the

Universe showing His extreme vulnerability to His inner core of trusted advisors and confidants. Through His righteous words and actions, Christ is the true and consummate embodiment of Christian leadership. He thought it important enough to communicate to the world that it is okay to show vulnerability. This is the same Christ who spoke with righteous authority, performed miracles, was willing to die on the cross for the sins of mankind, and spoke the Universe into existence. Yet, He wanted to tell us something about allowing oneself to be vulnerable. Jesus wanted to let us know that human beings have emotions and that it is okay to show those emotions in certain situations.

In John 11 above, Jesus was told that Lazarus was dead and was moved to tears when He saw Mary, Martha, and many other Jews weeping over the loss of their beloved friend. The entire mood was one of mourning and loss, which impacted our Savior's emotions. In the same chapter, we are told that Christ groaned in the spirit and was troubled.

> When Jesus therefore saw her weeping, and the Jews also weeping which came with her, he groaned in the spirit, and was troubled. (John 11:33)

There are many other examples in the New Testament of Christ allowing Himself to be vulnerable, especially in the context of prayer. We see in Luke 22 that—during His time of greatest anxiety, pressure, and oppression—He was willing to kneel down and pray near His followers.

> And he was withdrawn from them about a stone's cast, and kneeled down, and prayed, Saying, Father, if thou be willing, remove this cup from me: nevertheless not my will, but thine, be done. (Luke 22:41-42)

Christ was a strong, decisive, loving, and righteous leader who knew the importance of modeling the appropriate behaviors for other Christian leaders.

The world would argue that showing any sign of vulnerability would put the leader at risk of losing control of those who are following. They see vulnerability as weakness, a chink in the armor, and a human leadership flaw that would let others run roughshod over them.

Granted, I am not condoning an overly emotional leadership style in the workplace. However, there is nothing wrong with allowing our fellow employees to hear us talk about a need for prayer that will help give guidance and direction on a matter of critical importance. Neither is there anything wrong with leaders expressing certain emotions with tonality of speech, facial expressions, and a countenance that reflect the seriousness of a pending decision. I believe that such a demeanor has just the opposite effect of what the world fears might take place. Seeing a leader in a genuine state of concern or need from time to time will have the effect of rallying the team around that leader. It will motivate followers to take an active part in navigating and solving the challenges at hand. If they do not respond in such a way, they may not be a good fit for your team or the organizational culture that you are trying to cultivate.

Here are some other ways that leaders can allow glimpses of their vulnerabilities that can be used for modeling Christian leadership behavior:

- Leaders should allow their reliance on God to be evident.
- Leaders should admit their mistakes. "I was wrong. Will you forgive me for _____?"
- Leaders should allow their weaknesses to be evident.
- Leaders should allow for constructive criticism.
- Leaders should be upfront with followers when certain conditions are present in which "all hands on deck" are needed.
- Leaders should admit when they are having a bad day at work.

CHRISTIAN LEADERSHIP WORLDVIEW: PRINCIPLE #23

While followers want leaders who are unwavering, having a steady hand at the helm, they also want leaders who will show their vulnerabilities while at work. Because they desire relationships with those who lead them, they want to see evidences of a leader's true inner core to be able to understand them better and get to know them on a more personal level. Followers don't want perfect leaders. They want leaders who are honest, humble, genuine, and forthright.

24

COMMUNICATION EXCELLENCE

Communication—the human connection—is the key to per-sonal and career success.

—Paul J. Meyer

The backbone of any well-designed organizational structure (ministries included) begins with creating a process for infor-mation flow. Utilizing well-defined communication processes is another way for organizations and individuals to display high levels of quality.

When businesses and ministries are small, the need and concern for getting information into the hands of others is relatively small. One may start off with only five or six employees (or less) who share the same office space, so the dialogue and communication flow isn't a problem. At this stage of development, everyone is aware of major decisions and pending challenges and is experiencing frequent communication as part of a tightly knit group of employees. When you need approval or clari-fication from your boss—who is probably the founder of the company—you simply yell across the room. The company is still small enough where the communication flow is intimate, timely, and relatively easy to preserve the accuracy of the message.

However, as the organization begins to grow and expand, the dy-namics of internal communication will dramatically change. Otherwise, the loss of clarity in the communication and messaging with the em-ployees will put a strain on the ability to build solid teams for the long-term. This loss will limit the capacity for organizations to build trust and develop dynamic leaders while sustaining long-lasting results and impact. On the other hand, when everyone is kept in the loop with good communication flow, those organizations and their employees will have a better chance of flourishing!

Let's look at some of the building blocks of creating cohesive teams with effective communication.

VISION AND MISSION

Christian leaders must bring clarity to the vision, mission, goals, objectives, and action plans of their workplaces. Not only should they possess the strategic-thinking ability to articulate the purpose of why the organization exists in the first place, they must also display an aptitude for putting plans together (or overseeing them) for how things will be executed.

Vision

Most organizations that have great vision statements are usually those who understand the purpose for their existence. These visions are communicated in such a way that they express a lofty, motivating, and idealistic purpose for what they hope to accomplish as an organization. It usually points to a cause much bigger than itself.

Mission

The mission statement generally identifies the particular field in which you are operating and how you want to go about innovating and/or disrupting that segment of the business or industry. This is a statement that indicates how one wants to move the organization from point A to point B. It may also establish some overarching and quantifiable metrics and benchmarks as a guide for employees.

Goals

The goals that are established are important variables that should drive one toward the vision and mission statement. They are key strategic imperatives that, if reached, would dramatically change the landscape of both the company and the industry. Monthly reviews of the corresponding results compared to key goals are recommended.

Objectives

Objectives are the "to do" lists of lower levels of the organization that all roll up to larger segments and/or divisions of the company. In other words, each subcomponent of the organization will have things they will want to accomplish (weekly measures) that will impact the goals, mission, and vision of the entire company. Making sure that everyone has a rollup plan is vital to healthy organizations.

Action Plans

Action plans are the detailed activities you will undertake to reach your objectives. These, too, should have weekly measurable components and benchmarks from which to gauge ongoing progress.

OVERCOMMUNICATE

A Christian leader's ability to overcommunicate each of the steps above is a critical ingredient to organizational success and is one that must be given full attention. There must be a commitment to restate and rehearse dogmatically all the key elements of your plan. Each time a leader has an opportunity to speak—whether in large or small groups—some portion of the speech should detail a part of the vision and mission statement. The language of the vision and mission statements along with the underlying spirit must be communicated time and again. Some would say that the chief executive officer (CEO) should also be the "chief reminding officer (CRO)" of the organization. Ongoing emphasis like this helps to sustain desirable organizational behavior. In a sense, it keeps all employees grounded and focused on what activities and decisions are truly important by comparing them to the stated key drivers of the business.

CONTINUOUS FEEDBACK LOOP

If communication is going to be effective and reach everyone, Christian leaders must institute processes to ensure continuous feedback. First, the vital pieces of information must cascade down from senior leaders and make it to those on the ground level. Those of us who have been in the workplace for any amount of time know that this is much easier said than done.

Often, senior leaders will push down important pieces of communication only to find that others in positions of responsibility have either buried or dismissed the communication. Unfortunately, the flow of information stops and is dead on arrival. I call this the "silo effect" of communication. This happens when individual leaders feel they have the authority to censure what pieces of information get pushed downward. Senior leaders must never let this happen. When it does, there is potential for dozens of sub-levels within your organization to create varied messaging on key strategic issues. There should always be unity and conformity to what is being heard from the top. To make sure that everyone is receiving the same information, organizations should codify a formal communication process with appropriate checks and balances for compliance.

TRICKLE DOWN AND TRICKLE UP

The best way to ensure widespread messaging of aligned and congruent communication is to involve people in the decision-making process in the first place. Allow lower-level employees to weigh in and give their opinions on various key initiatives. Using those on the ground level as a sounding board can provide valuable insight that leaders at the top may not have considered before. It helps to give additional context while allowing employees a voice they never previously had. As discussed in previous chapters, involving others and asking for their opinions is a powerful motivator. Let's take a look at how the continuous feedback loop works when everyone is involved in the decision-making process. At a minimum, this process lets ground-level employees weigh in and voice their opinions in some capacity.

Trickle Down / Trickle Up Theory of Communication and Team Building

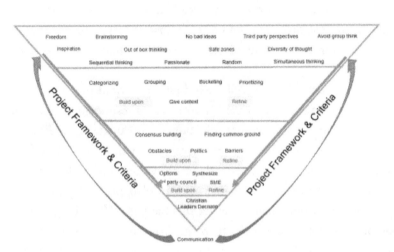

Brainstorming

The first phase of the inverted communication pyramid is where all of the brainstorming and employee involvement begins. Ground-level participation is needed to provide invaluable feedback. Everything goes. There are no "bad" opinions or ideas. There should be a free flow of information and continuous exchange of ideas. Ownership is created when everyone is involved in the process.

Categorize

Phase two in this schematic is where one begins to categorize ideas into key themes or "buckets." In this phase, one starts to pare down all of the various ideas into key categories that give the group workable and actionable items. In each of the first two phases of this process, the ground-level employees are still actively involved.

Consensus-Building

Once all of the key categories have been identified and articulated, the decision agenda is moved from the ground floor (sub-committee level) to the next level of leadership (full floor). This third phase of the inverted communication pyramid is where senior leaders get involved. Consensus-building takes place, and common ground is sought after. Senior leaders all want to weigh in at this third phase.

At this point in the process, Christian leaders must use much discernment. Protecting one's turf, politicizing various issues, grandstanding, and outright derailment of the process are all things that Christian leaders need to be mindful of and make the necessary course corrections, if needed. All through this process, the facilitator must ask God for wisdom, guidance, and strength to be able to navigate the decision-making and communication flow.

Wise Counsel

The fourth phase of this communication process allows leaders to seek outside expertise and third-party counsel. It is another way of ensuring that the decisions being made are the right ones. Getting wise counsel from trusted advisors is necessary. It may also make sense to seek the opinions of others outside of the organization or industry. The innovation experts out there tell us that seeing an issue from a totally different perspective helps to bring clarity, additional context, and may help spur on additional creativity.

Throughout the first four phases of the inverted communication pyramid, there is a continuous effort to refine, reshape, and build upon each of the ideas before rendering a final decision.

Decision

At the end of the process, the leader must make a decision. Once made, there should be thoughtful communication back through each level of the organization that is tightly scripted. Establishing report-back procedures at each level of the organization as part of the continuous feedback loop is vital.

When I think of how the Lord Jesus chose to communicate with His Apostles and create His Church, I believe that many of the elements in this chapter were present.

> And when it was day, he called unto him his disciples: and
> of them he chose twelve, whom also he named apostles.
> (Luke 6:13)

Creating a mission and vision for His followers, involving others, restating and over-communicating key points of doctrine, asking for others' opinions, and seeking wise counsel were all at the forefront of His messaging and communication strategy. Praise God we have His example to follow!

CHRISTIAN LEADERSHIP WORLDVIEW: PRINCIPLE #24

Christian leaders should provide the highest quality communication possible in the workplace. The substance and style of that communication should be above reproach. In an organizational setting, no one should be left behind from receiving timely and unfettered communication from those in positions of leadership and authority.

25

DISCIPLINED LIVING

There is only one sort of discipline—perfect discipline.

—GEORGE S. PATTON

Our Father who is in Heaven knew from the beginning of time the difficult circumstances Christians would encounter in the workplace. He knew that Christians would be persecuted and have their influence constrained while the enemy prospered under the humanist rules and regulations of workplace governance. God also knew that the enemy would try to muffle our evangelistic voices to the maximum extent possible. The workplace is such a wonderful proving ground and refining area to show our Christian love, dedication, power, and discipline (self-control).

In this chapter, we will explore the discipline of our Christian walk and testimony. When we are yielded to the Spirit of God, we should reflect an intense discipline while at work that shouldn't go unnoticed by our unsaved co-workers. It is a wonderful way to be able to proclaim "Christ in us."

The Bible says, "For God hath not given us the spirit of fear; but of power, and of love, and of a sound mind" (2 Tim. 1:7). Operating with a sound mind at work incorporates many variables and aspects of Christianity that include discipline, prudence, discretion, and self-control. Our co-workers can immediately distinguish between leaders who exercise these leadership traits and those who do not.

There are two prevailing management philosophies in the workplace right now: 1) order and discipline, and 2) disorder and confusion.

It is uncanny how one of these workplace philosophies lines up squarely with worldly and humanist thinking. I have found that one of the easiest ways to understand the elements of what a sound mind represents in the workplace is to lay out and define its opposite meaning.

The world operates with a very different set of leadership conditions that runs contrary to the idea of having a sound mind. They want to suppress sound and disciplined thinking and do it in ways that condition the mind toward randomness. In many institutions today, there is a leaning toward the democratization of authority, random decision-making, relativist values, confusion, and the belief that truth is what you make of it. It's like they want a workplace melting pot of undisciplined conditions, ideas, and values that fly in the face of a sober and disciplined mind. Yes, I do believe in diversity of thought as long as it is organized in a way that brings discipline that honors the Lord.

For example, there is a trend in the marketplace right now toward forgoing periodic performance reviews and evaluations. It amazes me how organizations are backing away from this previously held business practice that was once considered paramount to success. For as long as I can remember, performance reviews and yearly evaluations were an important part of most corporate cultures. Until recently, at least once a year, an employee would sit down with his/her boss to assess his/her job performance and what to do to get to the next level. It is a continuous improvement cycle that human resources departments embraced to the fullest.

However, there is now a movement away from holding employees directly accountable for workplace performance. This is done under the guise of newly instituted informal conversations that take place during the work year. In other words, the boss will conduct little "chats" with the employee to see how things are going. It is just like the little league team who doesn't know what the batting averages are or what the score of the game is. This is just one of the subtle differences relating to sound, disciplined, and sober thinking that is taking place at work. This approach points back to worldly standards where they don't want to see right and wrong (performance) but only that everyone is trying their best. This is a relativist and "everything goes" philosophy that will kill the quality and performance of today's institutions.

Below, I have listed some of the values and opinions that many workplace entities now embrace or will be incorporating.

- No bosses… only co-workers.
- No genders… only people and personages.
- No marriage… only same-sex relationships they want counted as marriage.
- No absolute truth… only truths that you say are so.
- No Christian distinctiveness… only humanist propaganda.
- No winning or losing… only participation.
- No admonition or correction… only an everything-goes, man-made culture.
- No order or discipline… only chaos, confusion, and random selection.

Fortunately, God has given most Christian leaders the wisdom and discernment to see through much of the vainglory of human reason and logic that is void of God in order to navigate the conditions of holy and righteous workplace living for His glory. We must be disciplined enough to reject all forms of doctrinal error at work while clinging to the divine moral precepts found in His Word. Going forward, Christians must choose whether to continue participating in businesses that spew the degenerate and immoral values of the world or to find a workplace home that allows them to live out their Christian values. In the meantime, we must fight to maintain the religious freedom we were afforded by our founding fathers. That freedom includes expressing and living out our Christian values in the workplace. It is said that there are many in this country who are trying to paint Christians and our associated way of life into the four walls of a church building. Christians should look around and take notice that this same thing is happening in the workplace.

While the Apostle Paul was encouraging his spiritual son in the faith (Timothy) in 1 Timothy 1:7, this verse has universal application for us today as Christian leaders. Barnes' commentary says,

> And of a sound mind - The Greek word denotes one of sober mind; a man of prudence and discretion. The state referred to here is that in which the mind is well balanced, and under right influences; in which it sees things in their just proportions and relations; in which it is not feverish and excited, but when everything is in its proper place. It was this state of mind which Timothy was exhorted to cultivate; this which Paul regarded as so necessary to the performance of the duties of his office. It is as needful now for the minister of religion as it was then.[1]

CHRISTIAN LEADERSHIP WORLDVIEW: PRINCIPLE #25

Christian leaders must be vigilant about redeeming the times while at work. We must put on the mind of Christ and exhibit such an uncommon level of discipline and sober living that the world will take notice. There should be order, self-control, and consistency to our thoughts, actions, and decisions at work. Being faithful and disciplined by living righteous lives unto the Lord is a great place to start.

---

[1] www.godvine.com/bible/2-timothy/1-7

26

WORKPLACE DILIGENCE

Learning is not attained by chance. It must be sought for with ardor and diligence.

—ABIGAIL ADAMS

L et's begin this chapter with a few straightforward questions. Do you care about your place of work? Do you *really* care? What are you currently doing to demonstrate that you care?

Be thou diligent to know the state of thy flocks, and look well to thy herds. (Prov. 27:23)

In all his wisdom, King Solomon understood the importance of being diligent in the workplace. For many back then, farming and shepherding were the predominant forms of employment and livelihood. It was an important way of life, and in many respects, that way of life is similar to our present-day workplace environments. Shepherds got up early in the morning, went off to work every day, provided for their families, and often traded their animals and other goods with others in the marketplace.

King Solomon knew that paying special attention and going the extra mile at work were vital factors in providing for their livelihoods. He didn't merely say, "Look to thy herds." No, he took it one step further to delineate the effort needed when taking care of the flocks and herds. He said, "Look *well* to thy herds." This is a call to awareness, care, and attentiveness that went well beyond the average responsibilities of the herdsmen. King Solomon was suggesting a level of care and concern that was extraordinary.

The same can be said of the care and concern that we should bring to our current places of business or ministry. When we walk through the doors in the morning, are we mindful to bring an extraordinary level of care and concern? Christians everywhere should be praying each day about how we can look "well" to our current workplace responsibilities. We must consider all the things we can do to fulfill the spirit and true meaning of this verse. It may mean volunteering for a project or work assignment that will cost us something. It may also mean spending an extra hour or two at work or potentially working on a Saturday to get caught up. There are numerous ways we can go the extra mile at work to show our care and concern as Christian leaders.

King Solomon points to the diligence needed to know the state of the flocks. *Merriam-Webster's Dictionary* defines *diligence* as "steady, earnest, and energetic effort: persevering application."[1] I see this as an ongoing and relentless pursuit of excellence with an exuberant attitude. Imagine an office full of employees who authentically have a relentless pursuit of excellence with exuberance. Imagine Christian leaders who were so excited about tending to their workplace responsibilities that they radiated energy and enthusiasm. Isn't this partly what King Solomon was alluding to when he used the words "diligent" and "well"?

Another aspect of diligence is the relentless and persevering nature to get something accomplished. Some would say that you just "keep on keeping on" for the glory of God. In *The Magic of Thinking Big*, David Schwartz indicates that "stick-ability is 95% ability."[2] The more diligent we are to sticking to something—instead of walking away or constantly changing direction—the more experience and ability we will gain as a result. It also reminds me of the charge that we find in *Hebrews*: "run with patience the race that is set before us" (Heb. 12:1). God expects us to keep moving forward, "running" for the cause of Christ.

Here are a few examples of the prayers we can offer to the Lord, requesting the strength to become more diligent at our places of employment and to "look well" to all of our workplace responsibilities. One should only pray these prayers if one really means them and desires to put them into action.

> Lord, I pray that I would be diligent in every aspect of my workplace responsibilities.

> Dear God, help me to be disciplined and persevering for You while at work.

> Heavenly Father, allow me to go the extra mile at work today with the enthusiasm and joy that would glorify Your name.

> Lord, I am asking you to allow me to be a good Christian testimony for the unsaved as a diligent workplace servant.

> Father, please help me to exude a Christ-like quality that impacts others while at work. I can't do this on my own while operating in the flesh.

> *Seest thou a man diligent in his business? he shall stand before kings; he shall not stand before mean men.*
>
> —PROVERBS 22:29

CHRISTIAN LEADERSHIP WORLDVIEW: PRINCIPLE #26

Christian leaders should persevere in the workplace with the energetic enthusiasm, care, and concern needed to show praise to the Savior. We must be willing to do more than what is asked and required. The oversight and commitment that we show at work should be of the highest quality possible.

[1] www.merriam-webster.com/dictionary/diligence

[2] https://idea-sandbox.com/blog/stickability-95-of-ability

27

TRANSPARENCY

There is no persuasiveness more effectual than the transparency of a single heart, of a sincere life.

—JOSEPH BARBER LIGHTFOOT

Throughout this book, I have emphasized the critical nature of Christian leaders building relationships with others at work. When we build relationships, it opens numerous avenues for witnessing and pointing unbelievers to Jesus Christ. While I appreciate all believers who attempt any form of witnessing for our Lord, in the day and age in which we live, relationship-building is paramount to success. The one-on-one interaction and engagement creates the level of bonding and trust required to lead others to Christ. While I understand that God can use any form of witnessing because He is the One who calls people to Himself, using common-sense and effective ways of reaching others through relationships in our current culture must be a priority. Human beings want to be able to trust those with whom they interact, especially when it comes to something as personal and life-changing as one's faith.

Let's consider one of the approaches that the Apostle Paul used when getting to know the people to whom he was preaching, teaching, and ministering. I call this the open-book-accounting approach to helping Christian leaders build long-lasting relationships. When I read the Bible, I get a real sense that I know more about the Apostle Paul (besides Christ) than any other person mentioned in God's Word. Paul had no qualms about telling it like it is and laying his life story wide open for others to see.

> Circumcised the eighth day, of the stock of Israel, of the tribe of Benjamin, A Hebrew of the Hebrews; as touching the law, a Pharisee... (Phil. 3:5)

In other parts of the Bible, we hear explicit accounts of his entire life story, struggles and all. We read about his salvation experience, thorn in the flesh, trials and tribulations of the ministry, personality clashes, and his holistic views on the doctrines of the Christian faith. The Apostle Paul takes us on a highly intimate and personal journey of who he was as a believer and what he believed the mission of the Church to be.

I often imagine sitting with Paul and peppering him with questions about the early Church and its formation. When I do, I come away with a strong belief that I already know the man as a close and personal friend. I imagine the conversation to be easy, free-flowing, and full of joy, love, wisdom, and transparency as evidenced in the Bible about his character.

What does it mean to have an open-book-accounting style of leadership—that is, a transparent approach—and what is the associated impact while at work?

- There are no hidden agendas or secrets.
- There is honest dialogue—sometimes, brutally honest.
- It allows co-workers to get to know each other to the point where core beliefs and dispositions are exposed.
- It helps co-workers learn to be genuine and authentic.
- We let people see our respective life-long stories in real terms (nothing fake).
- It allows organizations to build an entirely new level of trust that leads to maximum efficiency.
- Over time, others in the organization will be more likely to value one's thoughts and opinions as important.

- This authentic style of leadership breaks down the walls of suspicion and insecurity.

I had the privilege of having lunch with a well-known Christian author in fundamental circles and was excited about the engagement. This author is well-respected and known for his wisdom and insight for helping others to lead holy and righteous lives unto the Lord. I didn't know what to expect as this was our first meeting. Just from reading his books, I knew I would be challenged and blessed from the interaction.

We met at a local restaurant, shook hands, and then sat down at our table. It was at this exact point in the conversation that this Christian man began telling me about the many things he struggles with as a believer. He shared personal detail with me within the first five minutes of our conversation that had the effect of leveling the playing field. Right off the bat, he began to be transparent with me about things he was working on and how the Lord was working in his life. At first, it took me aback. However, I quickly began to realize that the openness and transparency of the conversation made for deeper and more meaningful fellowship.

Well, you can guess the impact that it had on the rest of our time together. I went from seeing this mature Christian man in the faith as a larger-than-life figure to one with whom I could have honest and transparent conversation and fellowship. In a short period of time, we began building a level of trust and friendship that normally doesn't happen in a first meeting. As you can see, it made a lasting impression on me.

CHRISTIAN LEADERSHIP WORLDVIEW: PRINCIPLE #27

Being transparent at work can help one build an additional level of trust with co-workers. Allow them to get to know you. If we are going to build lasting relationships for the Lord while at work, they must be more than arms-length transactions with our fellow co-workers.

At the same time, we must be discerning about preserving an element of mystery concerning who we are as individuals. There are many personal things that shouldn't be shared with others at work. Ask the

Lord for the wisdom to show you how you can become more open and transparent to reach others.

28

CHOOSE WORDS CAREFULLY

Words have the power to build up and unite… and the power to tear down and destroy.

Christian marketplace leaders must be painfully aware of the power of the spoken and written word and the impact it can have in people's lives. How Christian leaders use their words will have a direct bearing on their ability to influence the workplace culture for Christ. The Bible says, "A word fitly spoken is like apples of gold in pictures of silver" (Prov. 25:11).

How many times have you wished that you could take back words that came out of your mouth? What about the scathing e-mail, text, or social media post you just launched? Isn't it disappointing and infuriating all at the same time? The old man in the flesh takes control in the moment, and we are left shaking our heads in utter disgust at ourselves. *Did I just say and do what I think I just said and did?* Yup, you did! A sharp retort, stinging comeback, misguided comment, or a word written in the heat of the moment or in the flurry of daily activity can have devastating consequences on our ability to lead.

Certainly, we can scurry around and muster the courage to ask for forgiveness from our co-workers, hoping and praying that it will be enough to make amends and satisfy the hurt. However, depending on the magnitude of the offense(s), it can leave a big chink in our Christian armor. We might try banging out the imperfection of the new and obvious chink, buffing and trying to smooth the rough surface, or even using a strong temporary filler or adhesive to make it look brand new. Unfortunately, the underlying strength and durability will have forever been changed. What we say and what we write must be carefully thought through, studied, and composed before delivering the message.

The first two bosses I had after graduating from college were on opposite ends of the management and leadership spectrum. The first was a "Theory X" management style all the way. There was never a pleasant conversation or pat on the back. It was all prickles and stings with the most biting words possible. The sarcasm and vitriol used by this person was unconscionable. He thought he could bully and intimidate me to higher standards of productivity. Well, it just so happened that, three years later, he was fired. His words and actions finally caught up to him.

The next manager assigned to our facility was a "Theory Y" type of leader. He encouraged, praised, corrected, and led with words and actions that were appreciated and understood. He was a very tough boss who demanded excellence, but he did it in a way that one wanted to knock down walls for him. He was the quintessential relationship builder, and his words complemented that passion and ability. Eventually, he became a highly successful president and leader of a large public organization.

In a different experience, I was a relatively new facility manager. For the previous two years, our team in Vermont had our heads down, stayed focused, and were grinding it out to make sure our facility was the best it could be. Each of us was fully determined to do his/her part to make a difference. By the third year, it finally happened! Our team was recognized for achieving two separate and significant milestones in the same year. The recognition took the form of an acknowledgment of a "perfect audit" and admission into the "President's Ring of Honor" club. Winning one was a big deal, and winning the second one in the same year was exceptional. We were overjoyed by our achievements and the corresponding recognition.

Looking back, what made the biggest impression on our team were not the plaques, dinners, or the extra bonus money. No, it wasn't the material things that made the difference. It was the power of both the spoken and written word that had the biggest impact. Our leaders went out of their way to publicly recognize the all-out effort put forth by our team. Then, they took it one step further. Each of the executives took the time to write a handwritten note of congratulations and thanks. The CEO, president, vice presidents, and district managers all made sure that we knew we were appreciated and valued as a team.

The personal handwritten note is an art form that has been replaced by technological substitutes that are uncensored, poorly constructed, curt, and with grammar that is unfit for preschool students. They are so commonplace that it is difficult to derive any special and meaningful significance or impact. Down through the ages, some of our best leaders have employed the practice of handwriting notes of thanks, sympathy, and encouragement. These leaders understood that a timely and fitting word is precious and pleasing to the soul.

Abraham Lincoln was a master of the handwritten personal message. Here is a letter that was sent to Ulysses Grant after he captured Vicksburg.

> I do not remember that you and I ever met personally. I write this now as a grateful acknowledgment for the almost inestimable service you have done the country. I wish to say a word further. When you first reached the vicinity of Vicksburg... I never had any faith, except a general hope that you knew better than I that the expedition could succeed... I feared it was a mistake. I now wish to make the personal acknowledgment that you were right, and I was wrong.[1]

I still have all of those handwritten letters of encouragement from the executives during my time as a facility manager these 25 years later. Yes, a positive handwritten note can be outrageously impactful for encouraging others and giving them the confidence to reach for maximum heights. Our words should reflect Jesus Christ.

Christian Leadership Worldview: Principle #28

God has given Christian leaders two methods for exercising true leadership. The spoken and written word are the ways that we inspire, teach, train, excite, and persuade others to action. Some would argue that brute force and oppression, dictatorship, would be considered a form of leadership. However, I believe that tearing down and destroying others is not true leadership. It's a chink in the leader's armor that needs to be changed by the Spirit of God.

---

[1] Donald T. Phillips, *Lincoln on Leadership: Executive Strategies for Tough Times* (New York: Business Plus, 1992).

29

Capturing an Audience

Writing is more about imagination than anything else. I fell in love with words. I fell in love with storytelling.

—Pat Conroy

The easiest way to capture the attention of a workplace audience is to learn to become a master storyteller for the glory of God. Storytelling is a gift from God, and it should be another part of the excellence that Christian leaders bring to workplace. It's a way for co-workers to see something beyond the ordinary and mundane. Hopefully, they will see a God-given gift that shouts forth the excellence of expression through story. Carol L. Birch writes,

> The most impor¹tant qualities shared among great story-tellers are that they remain true to themselves and true to their own style. They are present. They are natural while possessing great depth of feeling for stories and listeners. Their enthusiasm is contagious and affects listeners.[1]

Those who understand the mechanics of developing, crafting, and delivering an inspiring story to support a position will have much broader influence at work. We don't desire to persuade others so we can wield some self-centered, egotistical, and manipulative mind control. We persuade others through God-honoring stories that help to lead them to Christ and proclaim His righteousness.

That it might be fulfilled which was spoken by the prophet, saying, I will open my mouth in parables; I will utter things which have been kept secret from the foundation of the world. (Matt. 13:35)

When Jesus walked the face of this earth, He purposed in His heart to tell the greatest spiritual truths ever told. When doing so, He also determined that He would tell those spiritual truths through the greatest stories ever known to mankind. Christ boldly and emphatically communicated to the world His key points of doctrine relating to who He was, how people would react to His message, how they could spend an eternity in Heaven, and how they were to conduct themselves as believers. There were no flowery words or deep intellectual discourses. He communicated spiritual truths through plain-spoken storytelling done with parables. Christ used 52 parables to capture His audience and deliver the truths that He felt people needed to hear. Think about this for a minute… The Creator of this world decided that storytelling through parables was such an important communication vehicle to influence and persuade others that He made sure His Word contained 52 of them! To say that storytelling is "important" would be an understatement.

When properly told, a story has the power to make people feel things they have never experienced. It has the potential to bring one on a journey that opens the heart, mind, and soul to inspiring new levels of spiritual awareness and understanding. By incorporating analogies, illustrations, examples, and humor, we can enliven thoughts and experiences that lay dormant in the recesses of our minds. Sometimes, all our brains need is a little nudge in the right direction that forces us to consider another perspective, emotion, or realm while bringing us to places otherwise unexplored.

But the real power of story not only comes from bringing us to those places unknown. The real power and impact comes when the story is so moving and captivating that it forces us to do something. It is when our spiritual consciences become so convicted and exercised that we have no other option but to act. Telling a story can be like throwing gas on a fire. It has the potential to enflame such passion and energy that our conscience explodes with newness of thought and direction. Don't we all desire to gain the full attention of our co-workers? Don't we desire for each of them to see such an extraordinary difference in the totality of our Christian testimony in the workplace that they have no alternative other than to point to the Spirit of the living God in us?

Christian leaders must explore the power and freedom that storytelling brings to the workplace. Storytelling has a functional use for every aspect of business and organizational life. All one must do is to think through the countless opportunities one has to incorporate the use of storytelling in the everyday work environment. Whether for-profit, non-profit, ministry, or any other organizational entity, persuading others through the imagination of story will have lasting benefits.

As Christian leaders, storytelling helps us to cast a vision for the future. Isn't that one of the most important aspects of leadership responsibility? The benefit of leadership is not getting on the ground level and doing the work itself although sometimes getting on the ground level can be helpful. The value of leadership is charting a course filled with the promise of tomorrow. Show me a leader who can do that with language that is scientific, ordinary, and without story, and I will show you a leader who has few followers.

However, show me a leader who can create imagery through vibrant, strikingly unusual, and authentic language of persuasion through story, and I will show you a leader who will capture an audience. Even the most unassuming, dull, and wearisome personalities among us can move others with a well-constructed story. While the delivery itself may be void of flamboyant traits of charisma, stage presence, and enthusiasm, a good story will cut thought all of that and get to the heart of the matter.

Whether it is the thundering George Whitefield persuading his audience with exuberance and style or the monotone and prosaic reading of Jonathan Edwards who preached "Sinners in the Hands of an Angry God", a well-composed story will leave an indelible mark and impression. This is the totality of what good storytelling is all about. It takes us on a journey that pierces the heart, mind, and soul.

CHRISTIAN LEADERSHIP WORLDVIEW: PRINCIPLE #29

The fruits of storytelling have no limits or bounds. Our co-workers are hungry for something that will stimulate them toward things unseen and unknown. People want to be led at work with ideas and thoughts that lend themselves to inspiration, possibility, and hope. Becoming a master storyteller will help you to lead people to where they want to go. They simply want to be moved and inspired toward a cause greater than themselves. That cause is Jesus Christ, our Lord!

---

[1] Carol L. Birch, *The Whole Story Handbook, Using Imagery to Complete the Story Experience* (Little Rock, AR: August House Publishers, Inc., 2000).

30

TRUSTWORTHINESS

If the Lord says to give more than you think you are able to give, know that He will provide for you. Whether things are sailing smoothly or the bottom has dropped out, He is always trustworthy. You can count on Almighty God to keep His everlasting Word.

—CHARLES STANLEY

Building trust and having the ingredients associated with trustworthy character is the binding agent that undergirds successful organizations. It is impossible to be an effective leader at work without the trust of your followers. Everything hinges on trust. Where trust is lacking, suspicion, resentment, jealousy, and the excesses of a manipulative style of pseudo-leadership would ensue. There is no other course for organizations to take when they aren't built on the fundamental preconditions and absolute truth of what healthy organizations must represent. Yes, trust is the cornerstone of organizational behavior and leadership. A lack of trust will bring organizations to a screeching halt, stuck in the mediocrity of meaningless activity and never moving forward with the consensus, passion, and approval needed for significant contribution and results. Such organizations are left motionless and without the rudder necessary to persuade and cause the changes needed to fulfill our responsibilities in the marketplace.

How much more, then, should a child of God and Christian leader desire to build a reputation of being trustworthy? *Merriam-Webster's*

Dictionary defines *trustworthy* as "being worthy of confidence: dependable."[1] However, the dependability and confidence that we should be procuring at work doesn't originate from the goodness of mankind. The trust and confidence we must emanate at work comes from a saving knowledge of Jesus Christ. We know that man will always disappoint us in the flesh. Mankind is wired that way because of the Adamic sin nature within.

> The heart is deceitful above all things, and desperately wicked: who can know it? (Jer. 17:9)

Yes, we trust in God. We also trust that, once we are saved, the Spirit of God will possess us so that others will see those trustworthy qualities in our godly character. We want our peers, co-workers, and others who follow us to stand up and say, "We trust him/her implicitly." Is there a better way to proclaim the name of Jesus with our actions than to live out our faith in a trustworthy manner that imitates our Lord?

What are the attributes that help to define trustworthy character? How can we live out a life of trust in the workplace? While there are numerous ways for us to demonstrate our trustworthy character at work, I would like to point out what I believe to be the most essential elements:

TRUTH

We should never lie or stretch the truth. There are times when leaders feel that they are at liberty to tell portions of the truth and what they would call those "little white lies." This should never happen. If you can't tell the truth, remain silent on the subject until you are in a position to tell the truth.

RELIABILITY

We should always do what we say we're going to do. Don't say things that you know aren't going to happen. This is just another form of lying.

Say what you mean, and mean what you say! One should try to live up to his/her commitments with the full strength of their efforts.

COMMUNICATION

If unforeseen and/or uncontrollable circumstances present themselves, we should immediately communicate those circumstances to the affected parties. Transparency is the best policy. People will respond much better to changing circumstances when they are "in the know."

FRIENDSHIPS

We should conduct ourselves in such a way that people can count on us for counsel, advice, and mentoring. One knows when headway is being made with building trust at work when one hears the phrase, "Do you have a second?" This generally means that your co-workers are seeking your opinion (advice and consent).

EXAMPLE

We should lead by example. What we say should match our actions. And we must be careful and diligent concerning what we say and do in public. There is now a public record, and employees will expect leaders to comply with the spirit of their words and actions.

SYMPATHY

We should go the extra mile for our co-workers. When doing so, we send a message to our co-workers that we are in this thing together.

WORKHORSE

There are times when we need to show our followers that we have what it takes to get down in the trenches and grind it out. In other words, we should be known as people who work hard.

UPFRONT

Rather than being afraid, we should be able to share bad news in ways that honor the Lord. Things don't always go as planned. Poor performance, poor company results, layoffs, or other disappointing happenings at work can be tough news to deliver. Leaders learn to fight through the anxiety of delivering bad news and get the job done.

INFLUENCE

We should be tireless in our efforts to make a positive difference at work. Every day that we head home from work, we must ask ourselves, "Have I done my best to move the cause of the organization forward?"

CHRISTIAN LEADERSHIP WORLDVIEW: PRINCIPLE #30

In the end, our co-workers should remember us as faithful Christians and trustworthy leaders. Our thoughts, words, and actions should reflect the example of Christ. If possible, the trustworthy nature of our Christian character should enable us to stand alongside those giants of the faith listed in *Hebrews*, Chapter 11. While not faultless, these Christian giants persevered to the very end with uncompromising conviction, trust, and determination to do what is right.

---

[1] www.merriam-webster.com/dictionary/trustworthy

Part 6

KINGS PROVIDE

31

PLAN, FORECAST, AND ANTICIPATE

Fortune favors a prepared mind.

—LOUIS PASTEUR

In the previous two sections, I explained that one of the roles Christian leaders assume is that of a "royal priest." We then explored those functional workplace characteristics and activities that would help us to demonstrate our ability to sacrifice and proclaim while at work, which are the roles of a priest.

Likewise, as Christian "kings" in the marketplace, let's explore how we can fulfill this aspect of our roles as "kings." In this first chapter, we are going to look at ways we can *provide* for both the organizations and the people with whom we work. We are called to provide in ways that go above and beyond the call of duty, putting a seal of excellence on our vocational activities of provision.

> And hast made us unto our God kings and priests: and we shall reign on the earth. (Rev. 5:10)

Leaders of any organizational structure will invariably become heavily involved in the planning, forecasting, and risk management aspects of the operation. It is a function of leadership that can't be avoided. Some would say that these credentials are the most important ones a leader can possess. I state this fact not to scare you into thinking that I am going to perform some "deep dive" into the components of economic forecasting and linear-regression analysis. No, I say this to impress on the minds of Christian leaders everywhere that great planning will put you on a bridge to somewhere. Likewise, poor planning will put you on a bridge to nowhere. As we have previously discussed, the Bible tells us that a requirement of a steward is to be found faithful (1 Cor. 4:2). I believe that part of our stewardship responsibilities as Christian leaders includes planning and strategizing for the future.

The first aspect of planning I would like for us to consider is the stringent analysis and study required before moving ahead with decisions. No matter what position that you are currently privileged to occupy at work, rigorous contemplation of all the issues is required when planning for the future. Given the complexity of today's marketplace, there is a plethora of key issues that must be weighed and balanced before moving ahead. Any single issue has the potential to be a stick of dynamite if not handled properly. In the business world, this is called "risk management." We can also describe this process as using patience, judgment, and good common sense before making decisions that will impact the future. Let's look to the book of *Proverbs* for some guidance on this subject.

> Then I saw, and considered it well: I looked upon it, and received instruction. (Prov. 24:32)

Leading up to the verse above, we get a picture of a slothful man's garden all grown over with weeds and thistles, surrounded by a stone wall that is in a state of major disrepair. These verses all set the stage for the lesson that the Lord is about to deliver. He wants our eyes to be wide open to the effects of slothfulness and to learn from this example by considering all the dynamics of the situation. The Lord is telling us to think about what just happened and why. He then proceeds to tell us to file what we have just learned away in our minds for future reference.

Isn't this what should happen when we are in various stages of planning in the workplace? Shouldn't we vet all the relevant issues and consider them well? And when we do consider the issues well, isn't the corresponding hope that we will receive instruction that will give us more wisdom and insight for forthcoming scenarios? Because it is impossible to travel back in time and change something, the instruction received must be tied to future action and decision-making.

The second aspect of planning that I would like us to consider is that of strategy development. This skill set represents an important element of the king's duty, which is to provide. We provide our organizations and co-workers with a keen understanding and knowledge of how to plan, strategize, and anticipate future events. Strategy is a military term representing a high-level plan to achieve one's goals under various conditions and levels of uncertainty. Strategic thinking is a systematic, organized, and holistic way of thinking through workplace issues. It can have both an internal and external dynamic. *Merriam-Webster's Dictionary* defines strategy as "the science and art of military command exercised to meet the enemy in combat under advantageous conditions."[1]

For those of us who spent decades in the for-profit world, our competitors would be our "enemies" in the context of the definition above. They make decisions and take actions that we consider, evaluate, and counter, if necessary. For those in the nonprofit world, other institutions competing for the same philanthropic share of wallet and subsequent donations might be the enemy. In the ministry, the enemy could be inefficiency, poor communication, and/or lack of timely follow-up with church members. In any case, we learn to be adept at maneuvering on the workplace battlefield with our minds, thinking for the betterment of our organizations.

There are many verses in Scripture that encourage us to have the foresight, intuition, awareness, and the anticipatory senses necessary to make good decisions. While these verses might not speak directly to the workplace, the application is broad enough to include every aspect of life, including the workplace.

A prudent man foreseeth the evil, and hideth himself: but the simple pass on, and are punished.

—PROVERBS 22:3

CHRISTIAN LEADERSHIP WORLDVIEW: PRINCIPLE #31

Please don't think that one needs an advanced degree to become good at planning and strategic thinking. Every employee has the potential to become good at anticipating and planning for future events at their current level in the organization. All one needs to do is consider Proverbs 24:32 and then voice an opinion of what to change and how to get there. The real effort comes when one steps out of his or her respective comfort zone and decides to help contribute in the area of planning.

---

[1] www.merriam-webster.com/dictionary/strategy

32

GOOD FINANCIAL STEWARDS

Let our advance worrying become advance thinking and planning.

—WINSTON CHURCHILL

All Christian leaders need to be on top of their game when it comes to good financial stewardship. There is nothing that can more quickly destroy an organization, ministry, or family than inattention or lack of concern for proper money management. I am so thankful that the Lord gave us proper guidance in this area through His Word. God didn't give us just a few passing words or innocuous verses for us to consider regarding our finances. No, He gave Christians a comprehensive roadmap to financial success (e.g. investments, giving, tithing, accumulating wealth, stewardship, borrowing, debt, co-signing for others, and family responsibility). When we come to the realization that everything we have and exercise control over belongs to the Lord, we should fall prostrate before Him and beg for guidance with our finances.

> (A Psalm of David.) The earth is the LORD'S, and the fulness thereof; the world, and they that dwell therein. (Psa. 24:1)

First, we must come to a deep understanding that our duty is to actively and diligently direct the affairs of the things we have been given. There is zero ownership authority for mankind here on this Earth. As we have discussed previously, there are dominion, stewardship, and ambassadorship responsibilities as we sojourn here on Earth for a very brief period of time.

Does the fact that we have no ownership position lessen the obligation for which we are tasked? No, it does quite the opposite. If we have a deep and abiding faith that the God of the Universe gave to us specific instructions with a sacred responsibility to be prudent financial overseers, we need to get busy toward that end.

Let's consider how the following verses apply to our own organizations and how we can better guide, direct, and give counsel about finances. We will begin with the most fundamental learning and financial principle (tithing) provided in Scripture.

TITHING

> Honour the LORD with thy substance, and with the firstfruits of all thine increase: So shall thy barns be filled with plenty, and thy presses shall burst out with new wine. (Prov. 3:9-10)

FINANCIAL PLANNING

> For which of you, intending to build a tower, sitteth not down first, and counteth the cost, whether he have sufficient to finish it? (Luke 14:28)

PRIORITIES

> Happy is the man that findeth wisdom, and the man that getteth understanding. For the merchandise of it is better than the merchandise of silver, and the gain thereof than fine gold. (Prov. 3:13-14)

For the love of money is the root of all evil: which while some coveted after, they have erred from the faith, and pierced themselves through with many sorrows. (1 Tim. 6:10)

No man can serve two masters: for either he will hate the one, and love the other; or else he will hold to the one, and despise the other. Ye cannot serve God and mammon. (Matt. 6:24)

GOD'S WARNING

Lay not up for yourselves treasures upon earth, where moth and rust doth corrupt, and where thieves break through and steal. (Matt. 6:19)

TRUSTWORTHINESS

If therefore ye have not been faithful in the unrighteous mammon, who will commit to your trust the true riches? (Luke 16:11)

THE POOR

For the poor shall never cease out of the land: therefore I command thee, saying, Thou shalt open thine hand wide unto thy brother, to thy poor, and to thy needy, in thy land. (Deut. 15:11)

DEBT

The rich ruleth over the poor, and the borrower is servant to the lender. (Prov. 22:7)

The wicked borroweth, and payeth not again: but the righteous sheweth mercy, and giveth. (Psa. 37:21)

GREED:

And he said unto them, Take heed, and beware of covetousness: for a man's life consisteth not in the abundance of the things which he possesseth. (Luke 12:15)

CONTENTMENT:

Not that I speak in respect of want: for I have learned, in whatsoever state I am, therewith to be content. (Phil. 4:11)

LABOR

He that tilleth his land shall be satisfied with bread: but he that followeth vain persons is void of understanding. (Prov. 12:11)

While these verses are in no way intended to be an exhaustive list on financial management, they give us the anchors needed from which to explore these concepts further.

There are some practical things I would also like to share with you from my personal experiences in the workplace and at home. I have found that marketplace Christian leaders should...

- Learn the value of money.
- Learn the impact of money.
- Learn the deception of money.
- Live below your means, both personally and organizationally.
- Learn how to tithe and give beyond that Biblical 10% standard.

- Apply Biblical financial stewardship to your marketplace business practices.
- Be slow and prayerful about making large purchases at home or at work.

CHRISTIAN LEADERSHIP WORLDVIEW: PRINCIPLE #32

God has decided to use our finances as a proving ground for Christian leadership commitment and responsibility. Our ability to use and direct our finances skillfully says much about us in the spiritual realm and other aspects of life. A simplified motto on finances would be to work hard, make money, spend less, and give to the Lord as much as you can.

33

IDENTIFY THE BURNING PLATFORM ISSUES

Marketplace leaders have a responsibility to provide their followers with sustainable economic, emotional, and spiritual value.

You may have noticed that the first three chapters of this section of the book all relate directly or indirectly to proper planning. When we put planning in its proper context, we see it as one of the vital activities that drives great organizations forward. In this chapter, we'll explore the importance of focusing on the right priorities of the workplace. We'll consider how we can sift through the endless distractions that keep us away from the "why" our organizations exist in the first place, while placing our focus on the items of greatest importance. There is so little time and so much to get accomplished in a work week that our process of prioritization becomes a critical link in the success of the business or ministry.

When I think back to my corporate experiences when I was leading sales teams, the memory that hits me most is how much time we spent doing unnecessary busy work. For example, a day wouldn't go by without me fielding a minimum of 150-200 emails. I did this in addition to spending time coaching the sales team, visiting major customers, hiring, and navigating the internal pricing landscape with our corporate office. I realized early on in my role as Vice President of Sales (Northern Division) that I was going to have to make a change if I was going to see my family at all.

My assistant and I got together and brainstormed a solution that would help me to identify the burning platform issues in my inbox. We decided to give her access to my emails when I was on the road. Twice a day, we would review the laundry list of emails that I had in my inbox. We set up three folders with the following titles: "now," "maybe," and "never." The e-mails that ended up in the "never" folder were immediately deleted. I figured if I made a mistake and deleted something important, they would eventually send a follow-up email or pick up the phone and call me. The "maybe" folder consisted of things that I needed to handle but not right away. The "now" folder was the one that I had to keep an eye on and manage. They were the emails that required immediate action. The beauty of this simplistic approach was that, instead of getting back to the office after a long day on the road at 5 p.m. and filtering through 150 emails, I now had my working list of 20 to 30 priorities that I could work through. I had my burning platform list. It saved me countless hours at work and got me home to my family at a decent hour.

While this example explains a process to prioritize something as insignificant as emails, there are other more compelling issues that Christian leaders must wrestle with at work. Strategy, governance, human resources, finance, sales and marketing, and cost control should dominate the preponderance of our time. How should we filter through the organizational noise and clutter that we deal with each day to move our employees and the organizations we work for to another level of proper prioritization?

VALUE

We should eliminate anything that doesn't yield additional value to the mission and vision of the organization. If what one is working on does not complement the "why" of the organization's existence, it should be abandoned. As Christian leaders, this will require us to make tough choices. There are many "fiefdoms" out there that coworkers may want to hold on to. You have probably heard the expression, "We have always done it that way." It may take some time, but be steadfast in your determination to winnow down the priorities to match your true purpose.

URGENT CHANGE

Focus on the top priorities that need change right now. They are the issues in the organization that may have dragged on for years that have left a crater-sized hole in the organization's performance. Take the bull by the horns, and lead your coworkers to a safe place. Immediate change should not imply panic but rather a logical and rational analysis of the strategic imperatives in your organization that must be hit head on.

MEANINGFUL CHANGE

We must zero in on the change needed with the major components of how the organization is being run. Leaders should not be afraid to suggest alternative models of success provided the due diligence has been performed. I'm not talking about change for the sake of change. The change that I am suggesting could be related to process, structure, strategy, or even cultural shifts in the way that employees relate to one another.

ATTITUDE CHANGE

Change will not happen without the attitudinal and behavioral change of the employees. When the burning platform issues have been identified and deployed, employees will need to step up and make things happen. Expectations will have to be communicated, and training must be deployed along with timely checkups on how things are progressing. Those checkups can take the form of townhall-style meetings, small-group settings, or in a more intimate one-on-one format.

I hope that these four categories have helped you to deconstruct and define the variables of a simplistic prioritization model. As I think back to Scripture and the burning platform issues of the day for Jesus, I would like to offer three verses in the Bible for consideration and discussion.

> Jesus saith unto him, I am the way, the truth, and the life: no man cometh unto the Father but by me. (John 14:6)

> And saying, The time is fulfilled, and the kingdom of God is at hand: repent ye, and believe the gospel. (Mark 1:15)

> (For he saith, I have heard thee in a time accepted, and in the day of salvation have I succoured thee: behold, now is the accepted time; behold, now is the day of salvation.) (2 Cor. 6:2)

CHRISTIAN LEADERSHIP WORLDVIEW: PRINCIPLE #33

Christian leaders need to refrain from basking in the muck and mire of the unimportant, insignificant, and trivial details. We need to train our minds to identify the burning platform issues. When we do, we provide a level of insight that will help guide our employees and the organizations we work for toward sustainable economic, emotional, and spiritual value.

34

RISK TAKERS

The American economy has been built and sustained by risk-taking entrepreneurs whose pioneering ideas and hard work gave birth to flourishing businesses.

—MIKE PENCE

Nehemiah's miraculous effort in building the walls of Jerusalem in just 52 days was a feat that was fraught with the extreme elements of risk.

They which builded on the wall, and they that bare burdens, with those that laded, every one with one of his hands wrought in the work, and with the other hand held a weapon. (Neh. 4:17)

It seemed like Nehemiah was dealing with every conceivable form of risk known to mankind. The risk of failure, political risk, economic risk, personal risk, financial risk, and spiritual risk were all part of that momentous undertaking. Notice also the steadfast activism and engagement of those men and women, which resulted in the growth and maturity of the nation of Israel. Their unrelenting determination and tolerance for taking risks produced the desired results and much more. In this example, we have been given a model for taking risk and then maneuvering in the aftermath of the decision. Using Nehemiah's risk-taking model as the backdrop, let's continue our discussion on risk-taking in the workplace.

If we are going to enlarge and bolster our dimensions of effective leadership at work, we must learn to take calculated risks. I realize that our willingness to take risks is dependent on our risk tolerance. That's okay. Everyone needs to decide for themselves what level of risk they feel comfortable with taking. There are many factors to consider when weighing the potential risks of a decision or action. Risk tolerance may also show itself differently depending on the environment you are operating in, potential downside impacts, your upbringing and background, your aspirations, your emotional attachment to the issue being deliberated, and whether the risk is organizational or personal in nature.

From firsthand experience and without hesitation, I can say that I am much more risk-averse when making family and personal decisions—especially when it comes to money—compared to making decisions out in the workplace. While I wouldn't call myself hasty or imprudent in the way I approach risk in the workplace, there is just more of a willingness on my part to take additional calculated risk. This probably stems from my upbringing.

Everyone is hardwired differently when it comes to risk-taking. However, beyond the differences of risk tolerance, there are three things that every Christian leader should be aware of and share in this regard.

ACTIVISM AND ENGAGEMENT

The first and most obvious position is that Christian leaders can't stand still. We must take on organizational risk at some level if we are to provide any value. If you think you can be an effective leader while sitting on the treadmill of organizational life and being a bystander, you are gravely mistaken. Anything worth doing in this life for the Lord will involve risk-taking. Remember that we are trying to impact the workplace culture for Christ by moving it from point A to point B. Change and decision-making require an element of risk. When we stand up and involve ourselves in the process of change, we assume some degree of tolerance for risk. Not everyone likes risk, and those employees who don't may even feel a little pushed, prodded, and elbowed in the gut toward a place they don't want to go. Nevertheless, Christian leaders must prod on!

To use a basketball analogy, we can look at risk-taking (creating change) like we are underneath the board on a basketball court, positioning ourselves to grab a rebound on a missed shot. We start using our elbows just enough to create a little room for ourselves, which gives us the separation needed to secure the rebound. We are not violently and indiscriminately swinging our elbows in any cruel, mean-spirited, or harmful way—at least, we shouldn't be. We do so to create the space needed to make a difference and help our team win.

In the same way, we use the activism and engagement necessary at work (sound reasoning and persuasion) to influence the outcome of the game. The poor rebounder at work—a person with zero risk tolerance—will sit idly by with his/her hands down by his/her sides, looking at all of the action on the court with little or no intent for involving themselves in the physicality of the game. There may be a variety of reasons why, none of which explain away or rationalize their gameday rebounding inaction. They may not have practiced or learned the proper rebounding techniques (study), trained hard enough (desire), made themselves available to the coach as a potential rebounder (instrument), or cultivated the confidence needed to get the job done (faith). Regardless, Christian leaders have a responsibility at work to take calculated risks for the good of their fellow employees and the organizations for whom they work.

MATURITY AND GROWTH

The true benefit of risk-taking only comes from experiencing and living through the process of change itself. It is the risk-taking journey at work that will bring us the levels of spiritual maturity and growth we desire. One can't say, "I have taken risks; therefore, I am." Rather, the risk-taker must postulate, "I have taken risks; therefore, I am becoming." We learn, grow, and gain different experiences in life (and at work) that help us learn to be better witnesses for our Lord and Savior, Jesus Christ. We step out of our comfort zones, take risks, and look to the Lord for Him to give us an additional measure of maturity and growth.

IMPACT

We should always have our eyes on the prize of the high calling of Jesus Christ our Lord. Every risk-taking decision we make that results in the corresponding changes should be done with a God consciousness so present that we are without doubt. Each day we go to work, we should expect to make an impact. We should have confidence in the impact of our decisions because we have fervently counted the cost with godly calculation. We place our trust in the Lord that He will guide and direct our efforts for His glory. The risk-taking decisions we make should be full of the patience, wisdom, and godly insight needed to leave Christ's markers on our places of business or ministry.

CHRISTIAN LEADERSHIP WORLDVIEW: PRINCIPLE #34

Christian leaders at work need to stand up, "quit you like men" (1 Cor. 16:13), and take the necessary risks needed to *provide* for the well-being of our employees and organizations. Our co-workers are looking for us to lead the way. They want us to make those tough and company/ministry-altering decisions that lead us to godly excellence.

Will you step out onto the basketball court, create some space, grab a rebound, and lead?

35

THINK BIG

Brother, you ought to take that head of yours, oil it and rub the dust off and begin to use it as God has always expected you would.

—A.W. TOZER

In the day in which we live in America, God has graciously provided most of us with all of the comforts of life to make our time here on Earth joyful and pleasant. For the most part, safety, security, health, comfort, luxury, and the liberty to say and do what we want—within legal limits, of course—are all a part of this blessed privilege. In many respects, we want for nothing at all. When we look around and contemplate our state, we realize that we have been greatly blessed beyond all imagination.

But what happens when we start to take things for granted and become complacent concerning those gifts that we have been so richly blessed with? Do we take our eyes off the Lord and sink back into the realm of the ordinary? Is there great danger lying below the surface of letting the shine and polish of this world's system and offerings confine us to worldly expectations, divorcing us from the consistent use of heavenly imagination and thought? Do we begin submerging into an unrighteous and unholy sphere where "let's not rock the boat" or "it ain't broke so don't fix it" satisfies our earthly and our spiritual longings? Could the same things be said of our workplace duty and responsibility? Are we satisfied, complacent, and stuck in the mud of the daily workplace grind? Or, do we look to the Word of God to remind us of our duty to "think big" and move beyond the realm of what is humanly possible or convenient?

> And Jesus said unto them, Because of your unbelief: for verily I say unto you, If ye have faith as a mustard seed, ye shall say unto this mountain, Remove hence to yonder place; and it shall remove; and nothing shall be impossible unto you. (Matt. 17:20)

Christian leaders need to throw off the shackles of anything that constrains our ability and capacity to "think big" and imagine. We need to believe by faith that God can use us in mighty ways in the workplace.

To use a sports metaphor, many of us have fallen into the domain of "small ball" thinking. This is a workplace environment in which we do just enough to get by, unwilling to explore the depths and range of Christian leadership possibilities. We have unknowingly painted ourselves into corners where the biases of limited and curtailed thinking reign supreme. It is a comfortable and easy place to dwell, no doubt. Unfortunately, it is a place that weakens the impact we hope to have for the Kingdom of God.

Let's now consider those life-long pursuits that will help us "think big" and move us closer to a *Christian leadership worldview*.

READING

If one is to aspire to a higher level of critical thinking as a Christian leader, one must regard reading as a constant companion. It is a tool that hones our skills for creative thought and imagination. It allows us to build and refine frames of reference that we might not otherwise experience. Our relationship to books should be of the utmost importance. Every spare minute should be devoted to improving ourselves through reading. In my opinion, this is not an option for true Christian leaders. Godly instruction through reading anchors and directs our thoughts and opinions.

WRITING

The ability to communicate to others with the written word will broaden our minds and expand our arsenal for the Lord. Writing is hard work. It forces one to think beyond the circumstantial and obvious notions of the way the world is ordered. At times, writing can take us to places that can be hard to describe. For example, the writing "zone" allows us to become acquaintances with ways of thinking that eventually turn into life-long friendships. Writing gives us the space to try on and filter various models of Christian leadership thinking against the foundation of God's Word. There are times when I am simply amazed at some of the things I have been able to write and wondered where it came from (both good and bad).

STUDYING

Christian leaders should desire to get all the education that one can afford. It doesn't mean that you become super-spiritual or super-intellectual. Learning is just another process to train and condition the mind. Studying is the art of conditioning the mind with knowledge and then using that knowledge in ways that help communicate logical and intelligible thoughts. In a sense, it helps procure specialization and order for our thought processes. The more one studies, the more one understands big-thinking and big-picture concepts.

JOB ROTATIONS

I encourage Christians in the workforce to be deliberate and calculating when it comes to making choices about which job rotation to take. The first step is to understand your own career calling. Be convinced that God has endowed you with specific skills and that you have a distinguishable bent toward a particular field. Then, through self-examination and counsel, one can round out needed areas of improvement with directed and meaningful job rotation experiences.

SEEK MENTORS

This is an area of leadership development where I could have been much more efficient during my career. It wasn't until the later stages of my career that I started surrounding myself with mentors who could offer sound advice and counsel. While there is always plenty of counsel going around in the corporate world, having the *right kind* of counsel is crucial to leadership development.

CHRISTIAN LEADERSHIP WORLDVIEW: PRINCIPLE #35

Christian leaders who can think though the myriad issues with high-level thoughts and perspectives are invaluable in the workplace. There will always be a seat at the table for those leaders who possess this skill set. This kind of thinking separates those in positions of leadership from those in the management ranks.

36

TALENTED CONFIDANTS

I hire people brighter than me and then I get out of their way.

—LEE IACOCCA

C hristian leadership involves selecting the right human capital to be included in the trusted inner circle of talented confidants in the workplace. It is like putting the pieces of a jigsaw puzzle together but with extensively more serious repercussions and consequences. When one starts building a team for the long-term, one should primarily be interested in employee fit. That fit includes much more than simply plugging someone into a vacant spot because the person interviewed well, went to the right college, got decent grades, and has the kinds of experience needed. I know what you are thinking... *That sounds like a perfect candidate to me.* It is certainly not appropriate to hire someone because they might be a friend of a friend. I know what you are thinking here, too... *But he is such a nice guy.* For far too long, businesses and ministries have hired this way, and it has come back to bite them.

The hiring process must be a rigorous one and take on a very serious tone. The hiring fit should include considerations based on one's ability to adapt to organizational culture, job demands, personal growth and leadership potential, skills sets, ability to get along, servant-leader qualities, decision-making skills, previous job performance, and the drive to see things through.

When I read about the organizational structure that was put into place in Exodus 18:21, it makes me realize that they, too, had a rigorous selection process that we can learn from.

Moreover thou shalt provide out of all the people able men, such as fear God, men of truth, hating covetousness; and place such over them, to be rulers of thousands, and rulers of hundreds, rulers of fifties, and rulers of tens. (Exod. 18:21)

At the beginning of the eighteenth chapter of Exodus, Jethro, Moses' father-in-law, had just arrived in the wilderness with Zipporah (Moses' wife) and his two sons. At the meeting, Moses rehearsed all that the Lord was doing for them and how He had greatly blessed them. They also took the opportunity to offer burnt sacrifices and offerings unto the Lord. The very next day, Jethro noticed something in the way Moses sat to judge the people that didn't seem quite appropriate to him. He told Moses that he was going to wear himself out by judging all the people from morning to night in lieu of all the other responsibilities he had. At this point, Jethro recommended to his son-in-law and to the leaders of Israel that there should be division of labor and a hierarchical structure put in place. The structure recommended by Jethro is a model of organizational behavior that still lives on today.

Let's now look at some of the "job fit" requirements that Jethro recommended to his son-in-law.

DIVERSITY

In the first portion of this verse, we see that Jethro was encouraging Moses to select leaders "out of all the people." He didn't tell him to choose potential leaders from one particular tribe or from families with a particular lineage or stock. He also didn't prescribe numbers (quotas) from a particular class or identity. Instead, he was looking for the most-qualified candidates for the job. He wanted them to look far and wide to select the right person instead of just plugging someone in to fill a void.

TALENTED

These rulers were to be "able men." They weren't to select novices for leadership positions of authority. These men—and in today's workforce, women, too—should possess the skills that are commensurate to the position. It wouldn't help Moses at all to select unqualified men who couldn't get the job done. That would have defeated the purpose of spreading the responsibilities of judging the people around to free up Moses' time. These selected leaders had to be the "best of the best" with their ability to produce results and relieve the burden that Moses was experiencing.

FEAR GOD

They had to fear God. How exciting is that? They had to be men who had the wisdom, knowledge, and humility to serve the Lord God Almighty. They were to exhibit a reverential fear that demonstrated their unwavering commitment to the Creator of the Universe. They were to be people who had the spiritual and moral courage to do what was right even in the face of adversity.

In today's workplace environment, much discernment needs to be exercised in this regard. There are legal protections against hiring someone for their religious creed and/or affiliation. However, hiring for "cultural fits" should include adherence to a moral and ethical code of standards that can be found in most company-sponsored handbooks. For Christians, that moral code is written on their hearts, and it should be easy for employers to connect the dots.

MEN OF TRUTH

These potential leaders should be those who crave and desire the knowledge, light, and truths given from above. They should live by the precepts and ordinances established by God. They should do so without duplicity or a lying tongue. They should have established themselves as honest and trustworthy men in their speech and in their actions.

HATING COVETOUSNESS

Jethro wasn't recommending leaders who were greedy or who coveted another person's possessions or position. He wanted those who were content with what they had and could make decisions outside of the tug of materialism or fleshly and worldly lust.

When individuals are selected for key positions of leadership, there is always danger that they could use the position in corrupt ways that feed the covetous eye. Jethro wanted to guard against this danger.

EXPERIENCE

The last piece of this jigsaw puzzle for selecting the right leaders included Jethro recommending varying levels of experience. Depending on their experience level, they would be able to be rulers over an increasing number of constituents or followers.

CHRISTIAN LEADERSHIP WORLDVIEW: PRINCIPLE #36

Christian leaders should be on the lookout for godly men and women who are talented, results-oriented, and independent thinkers and have a strong allegiance to the cause and vision of the organization. Organizations should establish a comprehensive process for hiring for cultural fit without exception. God's Word provides much insight on this subject.

37

BEING GRATEFUL

Talent is God given. Be humble. Fame is man-given. Be grateful. Conceit is self-given. Be careful.

—JOHN WOODEN

Have you ever noticed how much great leaders appreciate their followers and their associated contributions? They have the ability to say and do all the right things that show others how much they care. They do it in subtle ways that express their genuine thankfulness for the efforts put forth. Their timing is impeccable. Those who readily possess this disposition seem to know exactly when a word of congratulations and praise is warranted or needed. Great leaders also have a way of recognizing others for their work in ways that are pertinent and relevant for the moment. They do not offer empty and meaningless phrases that fall flat to the hearers. Instead, they offer worthwhile and useful praise that is pleasing to the recipients.

As I was writing this chapter, I couldn't help but think of the tremendous recognition that Christ gave to the Apostle Peter.

> That thou are Peter, and upon this rock I will build my church; and the gates of hell shall not prevail against it. (Matt. 16:18)

Peter was an apostle who displayed the highs and lows of character and faithfulness. The cock crowing, cutting off the ear of the soldier with the sword, and refusing to have Christ wash his feet are just a few examples of the impulsive decision-making and dubious actions that Peter displayed during Christ's ministry. Some would argue that Peter had one of the most impetuous, dogmatic, and wearying personalities of the inner circle in the early Church. Yet, Christ was able to see through the flaws of his humanity and immaturity to recognize that Peter was a man of action and decisiveness who would be needed to help build the Church.

Great leaders can often see through the deficiencies and inadequacies of their followers and are able to set their eyes on the respective goodness and potential of each one. Poor leaders, on the other hand, focus solely on the deficiencies and inadequacies, living with a "glass-half-empty" philosophy. I will admit that I have some work to do in this area.

What is particularly striking in the verse above is the extent to which Jesus was willing to recognize Peter's ability publicly. It wasn't a small gesture but one that displayed the full trust and confidence of the Savior in Peter's God-given ability as a leader. This is one of the most significant displays of gratefulness found in Scripture. God Almighty was telling Peter that he would be one of the primary instruments to build His Church!

How can we show our sincere and grateful appreciation for those with whom we work in the marketplace? We show appreciation not because the recognition is on the long checklist of good leadership practices but because, as Christian leaders, we genuinely care for others.

CONSISTENCY

We must take the time to celebrate the small successes and victories at work. While recognizing the major wins is always appropriate with those we lead, cultivating a workplace environment that enthusiastically recognizes the detail of the extra effort will help us to cultivate the habit of showing appreciation to others.

CREATING AND ACHIEVING

We should allow both the process of creating and the end result of achieving to be fun and enjoyable. Unfortunately, there are many hard-charging leaders out there in the workplace who are so focused on "grinding it out" to get results that they overlook the joy that should be experienced along the way. I am convinced that part of being grateful toward others at work is to create an atmosphere of joy, love, happiness, and fun.

PUBLIC AND PRIVATE

One shouldn't confine our sentiments of gratefulness at work to either the public or private spheres. It should be a combination of both. Christian leaders should build environments of gratefulness and appreciation, without their followers thinking it's time to get an "atta-boy" at the annual company meeting or party. On-going public and private expressions of work-related appreciation for specific acts of excellence should be cultivated. This should be a priority!

TWO WORDS

It may sound trite or trivial, but I believe that two of the most important words in the English dictionary are *thank you*! The further Christian leaders go up the ladder of responsibility, the more they will begin to understand the importance of giving a word of thanks. Often, leaders start to lose touch with lower levels of management based on their job responsibilities. The higher one climbs in the organization, the more weight one has when offering thanks and recognition for a job well done.

INCREASED RESPONSIBILITY

In any organizational structure, giving an employee a promotion with increased job responsibility is a clear way to signal thanks and appreciation. Assigning someone to a lateral position for means of additional learning, training, and experience can also be a great way to express gratefulness to those we lead.

LETTING THE HORSES RUN

During my corporate days, allowing my top-notch sales representatives the freedom to "do their own thing" was a form of displaying a grateful and thankful attitude. Those employees who consistently perform at high levels should be offered the freedom necessary to produce results without the restricting handcuffs of micro-management.

CULTURE

Christian leaders should be diligent about trying to build a culture of gratefulness. This will help to make the time at work much more edifying and pleasing to the soul. Creating workplace or ministry processes that support this end will bring unfathomable results and long-lasting loyalty.

CHRISTIAN LEADERSHIP WORLDVIEW: PRINCIPLE #37

Let's be honest. Are you truly grateful for your coworkers and boss(es)? As a Christian leader, have you consciously thought through and prayed about your responsibility to express genuine appreciation while at work? Is it a top priority for you? When praying in the morning, do you give thanks to the Lord for your coworkers and their unique strengths? When you do, this will become the first step in building the culture and embodiment of a grateful spirit.

38

DRIVING RESULTS

We get real results only in proportion to the real values we give.

—JAMES CASH PENNEY

Just in case all of you "type A" personalities out there thought I mistakenly forgot about the underlying reason that organizations exist in the first place, we will now turn our attention to driving results. Every organization has something they want to accomplish. As stated previously, our mission and vision statements should set the agenda for the things we desire to achieve. In the end, bottom-line results are what we are interested in for the Lord.

Results for leaders in the business sector may mean a higher-than-average return on invested capital. Nonprofits may desire to see growth in the average giving unit or want to top some aggressive yearly giving threshold. Ministry-minded organizations may want to see an increased number of conversions, baptisms, church memberships, or attendees in church services and programs. Regardless, we want to see movement (results) toward the goals and objectives that we feel will impact our respective organizational model and continue to give purpose to our existence.

Getting results is like a snowball gaining strength, velocity, and momentum as it rolls down the mountain. It can be the energy and life-blood in the midst of all of the toil, angst, and hardship of the responsibilities at work. Yes, work is tough and can be very taxing. However, part of the joy we experience at work happens when we start seeing the fruits of our labor. When the results start rolling in, they can provide an electrifying jolt to the culture and psyche of one's establishment.

The Apostle Paul was also an ardent believer in getting things done and producing results.

I press toward the mark for the prize of the high calling of God in Christ Jesus. (Phil. 3:14)

The Apostle Paul knew that living a selfless life of obedience unto the Lord, proclaiming the name of Jesus, and glorifying God with his thoughts, desires, motivations, and actions were the driving forces of life. The mission and vision of his life were clear: to win as many souls as possible and glorify God. His life's work revolved around these principles, and he put things into motion that would undergird and support each one. But how did he do it? How did he propose to reach the lost and dying world with the gospel message? The answer was Paul's relentless pursuit of driving results through others.

And the things that thou hast heard of me among many witnesses, the same commit thou to faithful men, who shall be able to teach others also. (2 Tim. 2:2)

Paul expected to drive the fulfillment of the Great Commission through others. He knew he was not a one-man show. Paul understood that Christ had designed the foundation of the Church and the underlying principles with a mind toward using the spiritual gifts of the entire Church body. As discussed in previous chapters, our unique and individual spiritual gift(s) complement, edify, and help to unite the Christian body of believers.

Now there are diversities of gifts, but the same spirit. And there are differences of administrations, but the same Lord. And there are diversities of operations, but it is the same God which worketh all in all. (1 Cor. 12:4-6)

Now ye are the body of Christ, and members in particular.
(1 Cor. 12:27)

Let's now relate Paul's example of driving results through others back to the workplace. First, Christian leaders must be active and tenacious drivers of results. We must be out in front, leading the charge and pushing the envelope forward. We must be hard-charging but with a kind and gentle hand.

Second, we must expect extraordinary performance from those we work with and from those who serve under us. Christian leaders should always expect the highest standards of performance in every aspect of work. There can't be any compromise on workplace quality and excellence.

Third, I agree with the old adage that we must "inspect what we expect." Telling people what to do or showing how to do it by modeling the behavior is simply not enough. Time and again, we must be willing to inspect our followers' work and hold them accountable for results. This also will help to make sure that our followers stay aligned with the core project objectives relating to the mission and vision.

Fourth, we must always be in a disciple-making mode similar to the Apostle Paul. Christian leaders in the workplace should have elaborate and extensive leadership training and development platforms. These platforms should be designed in ways that are easily accessible, create "safe zones" for learning, are challenging but realistic, and provide the additional tools necessary for increased learning and hands-on experience. Part of that disciple-making mode includes an on-going relationship (to some extent) and tie back between mentee and mentor. There should always be opportunity for advice, counsel, and communication between the mentee and mentor even years after the relationship was first initiated. Great leaders always find a way to stay in touch and interact with those they have influenced and mentored.

CHRISTIAN LEADERSHIP WORLDVIEW: PRINCIPLE #38

I can safely say that most experienced Christian leaders will find this chapter to be very helpful and reinforcing to what they already have in place in their organizations. They realize that getting results by developing people and building strong relationships is one of the cornerstones of strong organizational behavior and success. There is probably no more satisfying accomplishment that a Christian leader can leave behind than a legacy of being a disciple-maker. When done right, the spiritual results will flourish. Praise God in the highest!

39

STAY PASSIONATE

When you catch a glimpse of your potential, that's when passion is born.

—ZIG ZIGLAR

If one were to try and unlock the secret sauce of success in the workplace, staying passionate would have to make the top-five list of those specialized ingredients. Having passion is like hoisting a spiritual canopy over the workplace domain, enveloping everything it touches while penetrating deep into the soul of a business or ministry. It is a powerful, dominant, and controlling force that can motivate and exercise people toward a better version of themselves. Show me a man who is passionate about his work, and I will show you a leader who has the potential for greatness. Passion also helps to drive many of the other elements of leadership, so much so that it can't go unmentioned.

Passion is an element of our inner strength that is given to us by God. It helps to drive us forward with the excitement, enthusiasm, unrelenting zeal, and joy needed for the pursuit of godly excellence.

Passion is a mindset that one chooses to put on every day. We choose to put on the mind of Christ. Christians who choose to adorn themselves with passion will be blessed with an abundance of leadership opportunities in the workplace and beyond. Assuming one has an adequate level of competence, one's passion will be instrumental in helping to push him or her beyond the scope of what is humanly possible. Why? Because passion is contagious. It spreads like a pandemic with no possibility of a cure.

One way to relate the imagery and contagion of passion is to reflect back on that terrible day on September 11, 2001. One of the most vile and horrific events ever to take place within the shores of the United States of America occurred on that day. Death, misery, and despair were everywhere. We were shocked and perplexed that thoughts of such an evil and despicable nature could ever enter the minds of a human being. As a nation, we were heartbroken.

Unfortunately for the enemy, it also sent us reeling to explore more fully what it meant to be an American. When we did, the results of that exploration were both electrifying and unifying to our country. The citizens of the United States began to have a deepening passion for our country and for the things of the Lord. People were flocking to churches in droves and getting saved, while the renewed passion of being an American demonstrated itself in many visible and significant ways. It brought us together again as a country. For a time, the divisive nature of our communications was brought under control by a common passion. We were one nation under God! The unholy event seemed to propel us forward with a collective determination never before experienced by our generation.

The incomprehensible nature of passion can also be seen on the day of Pentecost when men and women were moved with a unique and special love for God and their neighbors. Let's look to the Scriptures and see how the day of Pentecost fully crystalized those passionate desires.

> And when the day of Pentecost was fully come, they were all with one accord in one place. And suddenly there came a sound from heaven as of a rushing mighty wind, and it filled all the house where they were sitting. (Acts 2:1-2)

> Then Peter said unto them, Repent, and be baptized every one of you in the name of Jesus Christ for the remission of sins, and ye shall receive the gift of the Holy Ghost. For the promise is unto you, and to your children, and to all that are afar off, even as many as the Lord our God shall call. And with many other words did he testify and exhort,

saying, Save yourselves from this untoward generation. Then they that gladly received his word were baptized: and the same day there were added unto them about three thousand souls. And they continued steadfastly in the apostles' doctrine and fellowship, and in breaking of bread, and in prayers. And fear came upon every soul: and many wonders and signs were done by the apostles. And all that believed were together, and had all things common; And sold their possessions and goods, and parted them to all men, as every man had need. And they, continuing daily with one accord in the temple, and breaking bread from house to house, did eat their meat with gladness and singleness of heart, Praising God, and having favour with all the people. And the Lord added to the church daily such as should be saved. (Acts 2:38-47)

In many ways, the effects of passion can mirror the things we see in revival. In revival, the Word of God—by the leading of the Holy Spirit—helps to bring us to another level of excitement, joy, confidence, enthusiasm, and unity for the things of God. While having passion in the workplace in no way compares to the significance of spiritual revival, it can highlight the "Christ in us" for the glory of God. As kings, this too allows us to "provide" for the people and the organizations that we work alongside. It helps to bring us to another level of Christian excellence.

CHRISTIAN LEADERSHIP WORLDVIEW: PRINCIPLE #39

The best way to illustrate the principle of passion in the workplace is to consider what it is not. Consider the attributes of a so-called leader who is lifeless, unmoving, lukewarm, and uninspiring in his or her approach to work. How would that workplace experience make you feel? Would you jump out of bed each morning and rush to work because you couldn't wait to get there? What about a leader who is passionate, competent, and inspiring? Passion is the spark that brings life and vibrancy to organizations.

40

TAKE INITIATIVE

Employers and business leaders need people who can think for themselves - who can take initiative and be the solution to problems.

—STEPHEN COVEY

D o you want to develop an exemplary reputation at work and be greatly appreciated by your bosses? If you do, be the person in the workplace who takes initiative. As I look back over my 33 years in the corporate world, there is nothing I appreciated more than an employee who was willing to take initiative. When one of my employees did something out of the ordinary and went beyond the call of duty, I took notice. If that person regularly took initiative throughout the work year, I would make sure it was documented on his or her yearly performance review. I also made sure that these employees were the first to be considered for promotions, raises, and other forms of special recognition. Taking initiative shows everyone that you care and are willing to do what it takes to make an impact at work. It shows senior management that you are interested in a long-term career rather than merely "punching the timeclock" for maintaining and holding a job.

As a leader, it is a pleasure not to have to instruct our employees concerning every detail and aspect of their workplace responsibilities. It is a breath of fresh air when someone steps up and takes initiative. Those who have been in positions of leadership know what I am talking about. Having an employee ask "What can I do to help?" is like hitting the boss over the head with a sledgehammer... but in a good way. These forward-thinking, energetic, and considerate employees know what it means to "get 'er done." They also share a common outlook about their workplace responsibilities.

SERVANT LEADERSHIP

Those who take initiative stand ready at a moment's notice to serve. They have an approach to the workplace that demonstrates true servant leadership. Initiative-minded employees are willing to forego what is easy, comfortable, and routine for the good of the organization by stepping up.

INSIGHT AND DISCERNMENT

Many initiative-minded employees have an acute understanding and awareness of how their unique skill sets fit into the overall mission and vision of the organization and want to do something about it. With discerning eyes, they look for ways in their given areas of expertise to "move the football forward" and make a difference. For them, complacency and inaction are not options.

FOLLOWER READINESS

Initiative-takers usually exemplify a level of aptitude and leadership capability that makes them ready for the next level of service. Because of their eagerness to serve, they put themselves in positions to be tapped for greater workplace responsibility and service.

DESIRE AND PASSION

Those who take initiative generally have an insatiable desire to compete and win. They refuse to sit idly by and bow to the idols of inaction and mediocrity. They repeatedly "go to the ant and consider her ways" (Prov. 6:6). Initiative-takers may not always feel like taking action, but they understand it is their solemn duty to do so.

COUNTING THE COST

They're smart enough to know that their initiative will cost them something. Service without sacrifice is like swimming upstream. It gets you nowhere.

On the flipside, there are some in the workplace who you have to drag around to get them to do anything at all. These types of individuals are not self-motivated, and it takes an excessive amount of time of holding their hands just to get them to meet minimum levels of performance. Leaders should have their "radars of discernment" held high for those employees who are running on cruise control with no desire to change their behavior. In these cases, leaders should be deliberate in helping them transition to other forms of employment with other organizations.

In the Bible, the Apostles Peter and John were outstanding examples of initiative-takers in the early Church. They were servant leaders, demonstrated high levels of insight and discernment, had high follower-readiness levels, were dominated by desire and passion from the Holy Spirit, and counted the cost of selfless service unto the Lord. They took the initiative to preach the gospel message of Christ in circumstances that were far less than favorable.

> And as they spake unto the people, the priests, and the captain of the temple, and the Sadducees, came upon them, Being grieved that they taught the people, and preached through Jesus the resurrection from the dead. And they laid hands on them, and put them in hold unto the next day: for it was now eventide. Howbeit many of them which heard the word believed; and the number of the men was about five thousand. (Acts 4:1-4)

The political and religious leaders of the day came down hard on Peter and John for preaching the gospel of Christ by throwing them in jail. However, their initiative and determination produced untold fruits. The Bible tells us that about 5,000 were saved that day. Consider how that one instance of initiative changed the course of the world. We will never know this side of Heaven the cascading effect and impact that those 5,000 had on generations to come for the Lord.

CHRISTIAN LEADERSHIP WORLDVIEW: PRINCIPLE #40

Christian leaders in the workplace learn to stay hungry and take initiative. We need to continue to plow the fields without knowing the entire conclusion of the matter. Our initiative-taking measures can open doors and leave indelible marks on the people and organizations with whom we work. We also have the potential to help change organizational culture by our actions. Will you determine to take initiative and make a difference for the Lord?

Part 7

KINGS PROTECT

41

NEVER COMPROMISE

The truth is incontrovertible. Malice may attack it, ignorance may deride it, but in the end, there it is.

—WINSTON CHURCHILL

In the last section of this book we are going to turn our attention to the king's responsibility to be a *protector* in the workplace. We should protect the people and the organizations with whom we work, patiently abiding in the shadow of His wings. We must also aggressively protect our Christian testimonies in how we interact with and lead others.

How excellent is thy lovingkindness, O God! therefore the children of men put their trust under the shadow of thy wings. (Psa. 36:7)

When Christian leaders trust in the Lord and are consumed with seeking out and living out His divine character while at work, they instinctively and by fiat engage in protective workplace decision-making and action. When looking to the Lord, the natural inclination—by the leading of Holy Spirit—to protect those around us will play itself out time and again. In secular institutions, we are trying to protect the sanctity and holiness of a community of laborers who are primarily agnostic or atheist in belief. Our responsibility is to stand firm and draw them back to Biblical standards of morality, ethics, and absolute truth. We must hold our ground and not let the Secular Humanists encroach on the righteous and holy standards of God Almighty. The Secular Humanist's religious doctrine should never be allowed to infiltrate and propagate our way of thinking.

Fortunately, we have many leadership tactics that can help us on our way. They are not tactics used to manipulate or promote disingenuous behavior but tactics that let our coworkers know that Christians use orderly, disciplined, and God-honoring principles and procedures when operating and leading in the workplace.

> But put ye on the Lord Jesus Christ, and make not provision for the flesh, to fulfill the lusts thereof.
> (Rom. 13:14)

This command represents a tall order for Christian leaders to live out, but it is one that should never be compromised. We must always put on the Lord Jesus Christ by emulating Him and never compromise the absolute truth found in God's Word through fleshly provision. There are countless opportunities at work to make provision for the flesh. Satan wants to appeal to the natural man and force us to a place of compromise. Satan desires for us to take that first baby step toward unholy thinking. He wants us to get comfortable with seemingly insignificant areas of compromise so we can take giant and evil leaps forward with indiscriminate behavior in the future. He wants to groom and condition the minds of Christians and non-Christians alike for future use. I pray this will never happen. We must resist the temptation of compromise at all costs!

If we are to portray an accurate and truthful picture of what the workplace is really like and to put it into proper context, we must face the unrelenting and searing pressure that Christian leaders encounter every day. The pressure comes from several different fronts all at the same time. First, we experience workplace pressure as a result of the spiritual warfare taking place. If possible, the world and Satan would happily have us conform to ungodly ways of thinking and acting at work. Satan has us in a "pressure cooker" for five out of seven days and desperately wants to maintain the ground he has gained thus far.

Second, we have the pressure of workplace cohabitation. We spend more time in the work realm than in any other spiritual domain. One has a job responsibility to interact with many of the same worldly personalities day after day. We all know how much of a struggle it can be to work side by side with those who don't share our values or beliefs. Quite frankly, it is easy to get on one another's nerves if we are not careful and prayerful.

Third, we have the pressure of job performance. We must perform at high levels, or we could find ourselves unemployed. There are even some circumstances in which we are performing at high levels and meeting our job responsibilities and duties yet still find ourselves unemployed.

Fourth, we have the pressure of providing for our families. As our families grow and expand, we are constantly looking for additional income streams to meet the financial demands at home.

I relate these pressures not to excuse any form of compromise but to reinforce our need to be reliant on the Lord in the face of extreme conditions. We should trust in Him to meet all our workplace needs and to confront the pressures we face.

> Trust in the LORD with all thine heart; and lean not unto thine own understanding. In all thy ways acknowledge him, and he shall direct thy paths. Be not wise in thine own eyes: fear the LORD, and depart from evil. It shall be health to thy navel, and marrow to thy bones. (Prov. 3:5-8)

I once heard a U.S. Senator make a comment about compromise during a speech at a prominent Christian college in the South. He boldly communicated his position about the art of compromise as he reflected on his duties as a U.S. Senator. He told us that we should never compromise; never! In his view, we should always look to identify areas of common ground but to compromise our Christian values and beliefs would be inexcusable and unnecessary. He mentioned to us that he believed he stood for something much bigger than passing individual pieces of government legislation with his name on it. He told us that he believed in the absolute truth of God's Word. It was an appealing and refreshing position for someone who works in an institution where compromise runs rampant. This U.S. Senator is a man who is a professing Christian believer and, by all appearances, dearly loves the Lord. Praise God!

CHRISTIAN LEADERSHIP WORLDVIEW: PRINCIPLE #41

Christian leaders should stand tall in the face of workplace temptations. We are going to be bombarded with the subtleties and deceit of worldly organizational practices and will be asked to compromise our Christian values and standards on a regular basis. That is the culture in which we currently live. The workplace is a breeding ground for this type of ungodly behavior. Christian leaders should be focused on redeeming the time (Eph. 5:16). We have been given the power from on high to be able to do so (Acts 1:8)!

42

BUY-IN VS. COMPLIANCE

Motivation is the art of getting people to do what you want them to do because they want to do it.

—DWIGHT D. EISENHOWER

Let's look at two varied leadership styles and decide which is most fitting for Christian leaders at work in our present culture. The discussion in this chapter boils down to two distinct styles that are at the opposite ends of leadership theory and application. One will help Christian leaders *protect* their workplace environments while the other has the potential to antagonize, divide, and destroy. One is centered on trust, people development, and vision while the other is centered on fear, paranoia, and control. While these two leadership styles are not anything new to organizational behavior and leadership, it is an important enough topic for us to consider its workplace impact.

The first leadership style is an approach that is demanding, forceful, and threatening. It shows itself in a way that often produces quick, short-term results but leads to dissatisfaction, division, and failure in the long-run. This first style of leadership demands compliance at all costs and leaves little to no room for self-expression or participation. It is a style that is void of any care, concern, and love for one's neighbors (i.e. co-workers). It is a selfish and internally focused style of leadership that satisfies fleshly desires. Here are some additional outward manifestations of what this style of leadership can create.

555

- Excessive demands
- Pressure
- Lack of trust
- Politics
- Dread
- Procrastination
- Nonperformance (long-term)

The second leadership style that we will explore is one that expects compliance but is done so in such a way that promotes follower buy-in, ownership, and a concern for the organization's mission and vision. In other words, it is a participatory style of leadership that begins with strong moral and spiritual authority while incorporating and communicating a clear vision for the future to its employees. Workers in the 21st century want to be led; they do not want to be bullied. They want to participate in the creation of something special that satisfies the "why" we do what we do! When properly administered, developed, and nurtured, this style of leadership will exude the following characteristics:

- Vision
- Encouragement
- Action
- Authority
- Teamwork
- Inspiration
- Goal-setting

Ultimately, this style of leadership is much closer to the way Christ led during His earthly ministry. Christ used a loving, encouraging, and vision-creating style of leadership. At the same time, He issued high expectations so we would conform to His image and bring glory to His name.

> And Jesus said unto them, Come ye after me, and I will make you to become fishers of men. (Mark 1:17)

In this verse, Christ was able to convey a grand and aspirational vision of what He wanted to accomplish here on Earth through the early disciples but with a godly authority that could not be denied. It is an authority that goes well beyond the confines of human and fleshly thinking. It's an authority consumed and enveloped by the wisdom only found in Heaven above. It is a wisdom with the sole purpose of glorifying the Father.

What better way to glorify the Father than to give man the free will to choose to participate! Man is free to take full ownership of the vision Christ has laid before us. There is no coercion or forced compliance, only a vision and hope for a brighter tomorrow for those who accept Him as Lord and Savior.

This same style of leadership can be useful for us at work as well. We lead through vision that originates from the power of the Spirit of God. We hope to inspire our followers at work to reach for the stars, never looking back or doubting.

CHRISTIAN LEADERSHIP WORLDVIEW: PRINCIPLE #42

As Christian leaders, we should ask the Lord to impress upon our hearts the need for us to be vision creators and not workplace destroyers through excessive and rigid demands that do nothing to build teamwork and cooperation for the future. We should incite the behavior and advantages that creating buy-in brings to the work environment to avoid the diminishing returns of forced cooperation.

43

WARMTH PLUS COMPETENCE

It's not uncommon for people to overvalue the importance of demonstrating their competence and power, often at the expense of demonstrating their warmth.

—AMY CUDDY

There are two necessary strands that run through every great Christian leader of our day. The first is warmth, and the second is competence. If a leader is deficient in either of these traits, the road ahead will be rocky and less than stellar. On the other hand, possessing both of these qualities will allow Christian leaders to lead people confidently and persuasively to positions of moral, ethical, and spiritual relevance at work.

Getting leaders to the point where they can master both of these characteristics is a lot of hard work. While it may seem that leaders are born with a natural predisposition toward relationship-building or have been blessed with extraordinary intellectual bandwidth, most leaders would argue that it takes much more than natural, God-given talent. They would argue that it requires a progressive and incremental approach to becoming fully qualified to lead. Christian leaders who want to help change the workplace culture must develop a spirit of excellence through diligent study, extreme discipline, and a willingness to become highly proficient in every aspect of the organization. Understanding how to master both the warmth and competence fronts is imperative to success.

Let's look to the Word of God for spiritual insight into each of these critical leadership characteristics.

WARMTH

> A man that hath friends must show himself friendly: and there is a friend that sticketh closer than a brother. (Prov. 18:24)

When I consider this verse and try to make practical application for leaders in the workplace, I am immediately reminded that not everyone has an outgoing, ingratiating, and charismatic personality. Those who have natural tendencies to be friendly and outgoing usually enjoy the "fuel" they receive from interacting with others and appear to be in their wheelhouse. I greatly admire leaders who seem to be "on" all the time. They have the ability to show themselves friendly with the ease and grace needed for each situation. Rather than being fake, it's genuine and authentic. However, for many of us, it is just not our spiritual bent.

I spent over 30 years in the sales realm and can tell you from firsthand experience that being ready to show oneself friendly with warmth at a moment's notice is difficult. How can we overcome the inadequacies and fear of demonstrating good conversational intelligence, friendliness, and warmth at work? It's not as difficult as it may seem if one incorporates the simple three-step formula below.

PRAY

Christian leaders need to learn to dig deep inside through earnest and heartfelt prayer and ask God to give us the right words to speak. We also need to pray that God will help us to speak these words in the right spirit. We must learn to pray and ask the Lord to fill us with the Spirit of God so we can exhibit a countenance and joy that speaks of the Savior inside.

There have been countless times over the years when I have prayed a prayer with four simple words: "Lord, please, help me." For me, it was a way to express a reliance on God in the moment rather than on any fleshly abilities I thought I might possess. It was much more than saying the right words; it was about being the right me.

BIBLE READING

Get to know who God is through His Word. Searching the scriptures on a daily basis to learn more about His warm and loving nature will help us to become more like Him. Generating warmth at work is much more than style; it's who one is at the core of his or her being.

PRACTICE

One needs to get better at the conversational domain through rigorous practice. Putting yourself out there in uncomfortable social situations can help you to practice and refine the discipline of conversational intelligence, friendliness, and warmth. When practicing, keep the following three things in mind.

1: Be approachable.

Don't stand around like a deer caught in the headlights. Smile and let those around you know that you are willing to engage in friendly conversation. Take some interest in the person you are talking with by asking questions about things he or she might enjoy. If people perceive you as being standoffish, it will be very difficult to practice and make any appreciable improvement.

2: Be caring.

Show them that you genuinely care. We must learn to love our neighbors (coworkers) as ourselves.

3: Study others.

A great way to become more proficient at conversational intelligence and exuding warmth is to watch how gifted and Spirit-filled men and women interact with others. The "hoary heads" at work can help us in this area. We can learn much about how they go about guiding the conversation in a way that is full of grace and love.

EDUCATION

There are many seminars, classes, and other forms of education available to help one get to the next level of personal communication and spiritual development.

COMPETENCE

> Not a novice, lest being lifted up with pride he fall into the condemnation of the devil. (1 Tim. 3:6)

While this verse is speaking of a spiritual overseer or shepherd in the context of a church body, it also has meaningful application for any organizational structure. Workplace leaders must be experienced in their trade, possessing the proper credentials. We have all heard the phrase, "He/she will grow into their job." That statement may be true in isolated circumstances and to a very limited extent. However, hiring a complete novice to a position of leadership is dangerous. For the most part, institutions need Christian leaders who have demonstrated a high level of excellence and mastery of their craft. Followers want leaders they can look up to, learn from, and count on to make informed decisions. They want leaders who have been tried and tested on the battlefield.

CHRISTIAN LEADERSHIP WORLDVIEW: PRINCIPLE #43

God wants us to be the best that we can be in every facet of organizational life. If one truly desires to be a well-rounded Christian leader (warmth plus competence), it is going to take a monumental amount of time, study, and training to reach those levels. It is going to take the all-consuming blend of spiritual insight, Christian love, and vocational expertise to reach the desired results.

44

DECISIVENESS

Pursue one great decisive aim with force and determination.

—CARL VON CLAUSEWITZ

I love being around decisive leaders in the workplace. They command the respect and confidence needed to get things done. They point their followers in the direction they want to go—after careful study, input, and analysis—and then make clear and concise decisions to support their position. Rarely will one see a good leader basking in the doldrums of inaction and idleness. Leaders who exhibit decisiveness have a hard time sitting on the proverbial fence with no movement forward. For these marketplace Christian leaders, the buck stops at their desk. They relish the opportunity to take decisive action that *protects* the long-term viability of the workplace environment.

In the Old Testament, we can look to Joshua as the epitome of one who acted in decisive ways.

> Then Joshua *commanded* the officers of the people, saying, Pass through the host, and command the people, saying, Prepare you victuals; for within three days ye shall pass over this Jordan, to go in to possess the land, which the Lord your God giveth you to possess it. (Josh. 1:10-11)

In the first chapter of Joshua, we witness God's transition of power from Moses to Joshua. Before the Lord handed over the full reins of power to Joshua, He gave to him one of the most significant pep talks recorded in the Bible as a springboard to conquering the land of Canaan. God wanted to make clear what His expectations were concerning the conquest. Immediately after God's encouragement, guidance, and direction, Joshua initiated the action documented. He assumed a position of supreme leadership authority over the people of Israel and then took immediate and decisive action to get things done. In fact, the book of *Joshua* is full of decisive words he used to motivate the people. Joshua was an experienced under-shepherd, had the respect of the people, was God's appointed leader, knew his calling, and acted decisively in the face of a daunting assignment.

What happens in the workplace when there is a void of decisive and action-oriented men and women? Some might call it "analysis paralysis." Everything comes to a grinding halt when leaders can't make decisions. There is a growing tendency in organizational behavior to "over socialize" key decisions when leaders want everyone in the boat with them when it starts to sink. For political reasons, there are leaders who will not take decisive action until they have 100% support from all stakeholders. They take themselves out of the realm of being a true leader and relegate themselves to a role of facilitation and cheerleading. They become lukewarm in their zeal for the mission and vision of the organization by bowing to the whims and sentiments of others, allowing other's opinions and influence to shackle the organization to indecision and inaction. As we have discussed previously, it's appropriate to seek the opinion of others, but ultimately, a decision must be made with or without unanimous consent. I believe that God approves of leaders who are decisive in nature rather than being procrastinators.

> I know thy works, that thou are neither cold nor hot: I would thou wert cold or hot. So then because thou art lukewarm, and neither cold nor hot, I will spew thee out of my mouth. (Rev. 3:15-16)

If God believed that having a lukewarm zeal for the things of the Lord was wrong, demonstrating passivity and indecision in the workplace can't garner much approbation either.

Which of the two responses below do you expect from a Christian leader after an appropriate period of reflection, input from others, and thorough analysis?

- "Well, I really don't know what to do because everyone doesn't seem to be on board with the direction I want to take."
- "After thoughtful consideration and prayer, this is the decision I have made, and here's why."

When leaders are seen as being wishy-washy, unable to pull the decision-making trigger, and carried about by every wind of change and opinion, they show forth a pedigree that is not conducive to decisive leadership. Christian leaders will command the respect of their followers when they stand up and take decisive action with authority. Remember that one must also support their decisions with godly wisdom received from above. That is what true leadership is all about.

CHRISTIAN LEADERSHIP WORLDVIEW: PRINCIPLE #44

There is nothing that a baseball coach hates more than for a hitter to take a called third strike. That means that the batter didn't attempt to take a swing at the ball before being called out and sent to the bench. He didn't help his teammates one bit by keeping the bat on his shoulder with indecision.

In any organizational setting, there will come a time when Christian leaders need to take a hard swing at the baseball, victorious or not. Decisiveness at work will set a distinct and unmistakable tone... one of action!

45

LEADING IN CRISIS

A man has no more character than he can command in a time of crisis.

—RALPH W. SOCKMAN

B ecause leading in crisis is so important for Christians in the workplace, we are going to revisit this topic using godly wisdom as our platform for discussion. Crisis environments can shake the foundations of organizational life and have lasting and sometimes catastrophic consequences. For some of us, leading in crisis situations at work feels like a daily occurrence. Everything is a fire drill. Our bosses say or do something in a meeting or in a casual conversation with a subordinate that ends up turning the entire department upside down. Senior leaders might read the latest article in a prominent business publication or hear about a new management technique that is in vogue, and the focus of the organization changes on a dime. The good organizations try to resist the urge of the "knee jerk" reaction and take a more disciplined approach to planning. Whatever the scenario, it is certain that one will face a crisis or two in the workplace. Christian leaders need to prepare for the eventual crisis with the corresponding wisdom necessary for proper navigation.

WISDOM

Why is having wisdom during crisis important?

Wisdom is the principal thing; therefore get wisdom: and with all thy getting get understanding. (Prov. 4:7)

If any of you lack wisdom, let him ask of God, that giveth to all men liberally, and upbraideth not; and it shall be given him. (Jas. 1:5)

When I read these two verses together, I get an impression that wisdom is important and leads to understanding and knowledge, that we should be asking God for the additional wisdom we need, and that God gives wisdom liberally to all who ask in prayer. When was the last time you had a crisis situation at work that immediately sent you to the Lord in prayer to ask for wisdom? Asking for godly wisdom at work can provide key insights into any crisis environment.

UNDERSTANDING

When we are hit with crisis at work, we need to be able to understand and discern all the issues quickly. Understanding how all the various facets of the crisis relate to one another will help us to make the right decisions. Part of understanding is thinking in logical, rational, and empathetic ways to be able to diagnose the elements of a crisis. One needs a panoramic view of the entire situation.

Another part of understanding is to be able to think fast and fail fast to make the necessary adjustments. In other words, if you chart a decision-making course that doesn't work out, you must be able to quickly think through and launch alternative problem-solving solutions.

RISK IMPACT

Once we have a full understanding of the issues, we must then go into risk-management mode to "protect" the organization and its employees. There could be financial, human capital, or branding concerns to contend with.

ENDURANCE

We must ask God to give us the wisdom to endure the hardships when they materialize. Most crisis situations elevate the level of stress and anxiety for those involved. Some bring unexpected degrees of change. We need to be able stay focused and work through the stress by relying on the Holy Spirit. In times like these, we must run to the wisdom of God and plead for assistance. Ask God to build a hedge of protection around your thinking.

PREPARATION

We must seek the wisdom of foresight to prepare adequately for the future. After figuring out the cause and the risk, Christian leaders then start looking to the future. They put action plans into place to curtail or eliminate any reoccurrence of the crisis. They also extract key learning information that will help codify responses to future crisis situations. While not every crisis is exactly the same, leaders should be able to find and establish common protocols and processes developed through the experience.

COMMUNICATION

Communication with employees during a crisis must be flawless. Everyone must be kept in the loop with consistent messaging. While the communication objective is listed as the fifth bullet point in this chapter, it must be pervasive throughout the entire process. One should employ a multimedia approach to making sure that everyone is kept in the loop with truthful and up-to-date information.

Looking back on my career, there are many examples that I could share with you relating to crisis situations that I went through. However, there was one specific circumstance early in my career that stands out. It happened when our workers went on strike. The strike happened over an extended period of time and was unnerving and unsettling to most of us. Customers were upset, salary reductions were enacted for managers, striking workers had no access to income, our company lost money, and the overall trust between management and the union went in the tank. To say that the situation was tense would be an understatement. It was a crisis.

What I remember most about how we handled the crisis was the level of communication we received from corporate. They were right on point when it came to giving us a blow-by-blow description of what was happening in the negotiations. They also kept our major customers well informed. We had talking points, videos, news bulletins, and other pieces of communication that we shared with both our customers and employees that had a lasting impact.

Once the strike was over, we heard time and again from our customers (via surveys) that they appreciated our efforts to communicate with them. While the management employees were not happy with the salary reductions, they also expressed appreciation for the clear and consistent communication during the crisis.

CHRISTIAN LEADERSHIP WORLDVIEW: PRINCIPLE #45

Christian leaders in the workplace should prepare right now for crisis situations. They should meet with their employees and talk through potential workplace scenarios and how they will respond in the event of a crisis. Each of the steps listed in this chapter should be considered, addressing multiple workplace scenarios. Ask God for the wisdom, knowledge, and understanding needed to say and do all the right things during crisis events. God will honor and bless your preparation.

46

COURSE CORRECTION

You cannot change your destination overnight, but you can change your direction overnight.

—JIM ROHN

G reat leaders adapt, change direction, and course correct with the foresight and anticipation needed for maximum results. Show me an organization that is doing the same things and performing the same tasks over and over without the capacity for change, and I will show you an organization that is on the road to expiration. Times change, people change, organizations change, markets change, and our culture changes. To stay relevant as an institution or entity, we must stay ready to change or be prepared to be left behind.

Now, I am not taking about change relating to different standards of absolute truth (Bible truth), morality, ethics, or godly standards of excellence. The Word of God should always reign supreme. His Word never changes. However, what I am referring to are different ways of thinking out of the box with creative and innovative approaches to the workplace. We must be willing to employ a matrix of different models of change and course correction to help bolster and "protect" our workplace for the long-term. We all know that change is good when done for the right reasons and when it aligns with the will of God.

In the Bible, God uses the word "turn" to represent a change of mind that leads to a change of direction. It is referring to a change that turns our attention, focus, and way of being toward the things of the Lord when accepting Him as Savior.

While the organizational change we will be addressing in this chapter is not in a spiritual sense, it also represents a change of mind that leads to a change of direction.

In his book, *Change by Design*, Tim Brown offers four different models through which we can think about change. We are going to adapt and modify some of his models to fit our discussion in this chapter.

MANAGE

Incrementally, move existing processes and ways of conducting business to new spheres of design and thinking. This is the slow and steady type of course correction that is the least disruptive and will cause the least amount of anxiety and heartburn. This approach is so far below the radar that most employees will not even recognize the change.

ADAPT

Seek alternative avenues with existing processes and ways of conducting business to new markets or groups of people we hope to impact with an exploratory and adapting approach. In other words, adapt what we already have to new groups.

EXTEND

Develop new offerings to existing processes and ways of conducting business by expanding the breadth of products and/or services. When organizations start to extend by creating new processes and ways of conducting business, they are moving to a more aggressive model of course correction and change. In this model, we have moved into the realm of creating something new and unique.

CREATE

Lastly, the riskiest design and course correction adventure would be to establish new offerings for new processes and ways of conducting business. Here, you are venturing into the world of massive change and disruptive innovation. Organizations who are in this sphere are either about to experience total failure (incorporate high degree of change or go out of business) or have revolutionary thinkers and strategists who can anticipate market needs.[1]

I have listed the modified versions of Brown's models to help us think about change through a lens that is progressive, logical, and systematic.

How should Christian leaders incorporate change into their places of work? For those who have a *Christian leadership worldview*, what are some of the spiritual elements of organizational change that we must consider in addition to the models of progressive change stated above?

First, we should never be afraid to make changes, whether small or large, when we are being led by the Holy Spirit to do so. If we are in His Word daily, enlightened and sensitive to the Spirit's leading, we need to proceed with the change.

Second, quickly walk through the doors that you are confident the Lord has opened for you, but stay away from the doors He closes tight. Don't try to pry the doors open or bust through them in the flesh. This is a human tendency that we can all display at times.

Third, there are times when God wants you to plow around an obstacle of change instead of going directly through it. In other words, learn to navigate change management with godly wisdom.

Fourth, change leaders learn how to take instruction well. They are so grounded and sure of their callings and positions of authority that they welcome advice and criticism from others. In fact, they enjoy the give and take of discussion and debate.

Fifth, marketplace leaders seek out diversity of opinion to make the necessary corrections. Clones ("yes" men) can be harmful to the efficient working of an organization.

Christian Leadership Worldview: Principle #46

Great organizations strive for continuous improvement in orderly and systematic ways. For that to happen, Christian leaders must be adept at managing and incorporating appropriate elements of course correction and change. It is a leader's responsibility and duty to know the answers to the who, what, when, where, how, and why of organizational change. Allow the Lord to lead!

---

[1] Tim Brown, *Change by Design* (New York: HarperCollins, 2009).

47

NEVER ABUSE AUTHORITY

Sin is the reason we abuse our authority.

—BENJAMIN WATSON

art of our responsibility as Christian leaders is not to let our baser human instincts control and dominate our methods and style of leading others. All too often, Christian leaders let down their spiritual guard and operate in the flesh in the workplace environment. There are even some extreme examples where leaders abuse their workplace authority. We must never let this happen. If we do, our reputations and testimonies for the Lord will be completely tarnished. Word will quickly spread around the office that you are a leader who operates on the wrong side of the tracks. Stories will be told, perceptions will be formed, gossip will abound, and your ability to impact others for Christ will be limited.

The Bible has a clear example of a leader who abused his authority. In many respects, King Saul demonstrated the miserable conditions of what could potentially happen when hearts are hardened. Below are some of the ungodly characteristics of King Saul that led to his abuse of authority found in the book of *First Samuel.*

- Pride
- Fear
- Anxiety
- Mean spiritedness
- Jealousy

- Covetousness
- Anger
- Resentment
- Personality conflicts
- Wrong priorities
- Paranoia

King Saul was the first king of Israel and seemed to have all of the right credentials. He was a tall, attractive man who came from the tribe of Benjamin. He showed himself strong in military battles and had the favor of several of the neighboring tribes. The Bible indicates that he stood head and shoulders above the average person, casting a "goodly personage" to all those around him. By all appearances, he was the right man for the job.

> Now there was a man of Benjamin, whose name was Kish, the son of Abiel, the son of Zeror, the son of Bechorath, the son of Aphiah, a Benjamite, a mighty man of power. And he had a son, whose name was Saul, a choice young man, and a goodly: and there was not among the children of Israel a goodlier person than he: from his shoulders and upward he was higher than any of the people. (1 Sam. 9:1-2)

Unfortunately, to know the real King Saul, we must diligently unpack the baser human instincts described earlier. When we uncover that he had an unrelenting quest for power and control, we begin to understand why he abused his authority. He could not let go and share the power and notoriety of being king. Every time his servant David did something that was praiseworthy, King Saul went into hyper-drive to destroy him. He became so obsessed with the destruction of David that King Saul had ongoing campaigns to box him in and corner him.

King Saul's passion for power and control didn't stop with David, either. His abuse of authority showed itself in the usurpation of the priest's duties as well. King Saul was so self-absorbed and had so little care and evidences of spiritual sensitivity that he decided to make the peace offerings and burnt offerings by himself.

Samuel was beside himself and asked, "What hast thou done?"

"And Saul said, Bring hither a burnt offering to me, and peace offerings. And he offered the burnt offering" (1 Sam. 13:9).

"And Samuel said to Saul, Thou hast done foolishly: thou hast not kept the commandment of the LORD thy God, which he commanded thee: for now would the LORD have established thy kingdom upon Israel for ever" (1 Sam. 13:13).

There are many ways that organizational leaders in the 21st century can also abuse their authority. Christian leaders must be aware of any wrong steps in these directions and immediately change course.

- False accusations
- Excessively demanding
- Inappropriate language
- Discriminatory practices
- Limit upward mobility
- Isolate
- Disenfranchise
- Humiliate
- Retaliate

CHRISTIAN LEADERSHIP WORLDVIEW: PRINCIPLE #47

If you ever find yourself out on the abuse-of-authority "limb" in the workplace, seek the help and guidance needed from trusted advisors. It is okay to take "leadership perception" baths once in a while to make sure you haven't strayed too far from the leadership principles found in God's Word. We are imperfect human beings serving a holy, righteous, and perfect God!

48

LIMITATION AWARENESS

The God we serve does not seek out the perfect, but instead uses our imperfections and our shortcomings for his greater good. I am humbled by my own limitations. But where I am weak, He is strong.

—RICK PERRY

Christian leaders should strive to have a proper understanding of their own limitations, set aside time for self-examination, and be willing to admit workplace shortcomings. When leaders critically examine their strengths and weaknesses, it gives them a distinct advantage for personal growth and the insight necessary for building healthy organizations.

People don't want to work for a know-it-all. There is nothing more frustrating than working for a boss who has everything already figured out. People love to work in environments where there is a melding of spiritual gifts and natural talents that strengthen the fiber of the organization. It's an environment that has complementary and cascading participation, eliminating or minimizing unnecessary defects and needless waste.

How am I doing? What do I need to improve? These are two terrific questions to ask one's coworkers and supervisors. They cut right to the bottom line of continuous improvement and signal to everyone that you are acknowledging your vocational limitations. This process should be as easy as apple pie. There should be no worries that you are opening yourself up to unnecessary critique, censure, or the possibility of being fired. On the contrary, by being forthcoming with your limitations, you are opening up a whole new world of possibilities.

If Christian leaders take the initiative to ask for help in specific areas of needed workplace improvement, this will demonstrate personal responsibility and the potential for assuming higher levels of organizational leadership and authority later on.

The Apostle Paul was very open about his limitations in the flesh yet was used mightily by God.

> And lest I should be exalted above measure through the abundance of the revelations, there was given to me a thorn in the flesh, the messenger of Satan to buffet me, lest I should be exalted above measure. (2 Cor. 12:7)

The Apostle Paul was one of the most sophisticated intellectuals and religious scholars of his day. He was the person God used to write a significant portion of the New Testament. Yet, God saw fit to give him a thorn in the flesh to remind him of his limited human capacity on Earth and of his need to rely on the Creator of this world. There may have been a propensity toward high-minded thinking or other improvement areas for Paul that the Lord wanted to reel in. The Bible doesn't specifically say what his thorn in the flesh was, but we do know that Paul was acutely aware of the importance of self-examination. The Lord used the Apostle Paul to remind us of our duty in the book of *First Corinthians* concerning the Lord's Supper.

> But let a man examine himself, and so let him eat of that bread, and drink of that cup. (1 Cor. 11:28)

The Lord's Supper is to be used as a solemn and serious time to remember our Lord and His atoning sacrifice on the Cross of Calvary. We are to root out and ask for forgiveness of any remnant of sin and iniquity that we have in our lives.

That same internally focused thought process of self-examination should be used by Christian leaders everywhere on a continual basis. In addition to leaders dealing with sin issues that they may be harboring, we also need to thoroughly explore and acknowledge workplace shortcomings. We need to ask ourselves, "Lord what do I need to learn, and what do You want to teach me here at work?" If one is self-aware and has the spiritual maturity and insight to perform such a check, the capacity to lead will be strengthened.

Alternatively, unattended blind spots can limit one's upward organizational mobility if not given serious attention. When senior leaders meet to discuss follower readiness levels, those with the unattended blind spots generally remain in their current positions of leadership. Sometimes, the nature and degree of those blind spots factor into the decision-making process of whether or not to promote. Leaders may see a small and insignificant leadership flaw that hasn't been dealt with and decide to go in another direction. That is why seeking the counsel of others is such an important thing to do even in the work environment.

Christian leadership coaches and mentors can help smooth out the rough edges that we may be unaware of relating to our leadership styles and help put us back on the right track. It is well worth the time, effort, and investment of securing a reliable and experienced Christian coach. It is never too late to ask for help.

I recently had a coaching experience from someone who I consider to be an experienced mentor. This person uncovered a blind spot in my life and helped point me in the right direction. While the coaching experience wasn't significant or life-altering, it was very relevant, sound, and logical counsel related to an issue of the CLWI ministry.

Identifying one's limitations or blind spots can be as easy or as hard as one makes it. Here is a simple five-step process.

WILLINGNESS

It all starts with having the humility and willingness to change. Christian leaders must be willing to let themselves be vulnerable and exposed to potential areas of limitation and weakness.

SEEK

Once the human spirit is willing, Christian leaders start actively seeking opportunities to look in the mirror through coaching and counsel.

UNDERSTAND AND ACKNOWLEDGE

As those opportunities for self-examination and reflection present themselves, Christian leaders should diligently seek wisdom from God to understand and acknowledge the limitation.

ACTION PLAN

This is the step in the process where a plan is enacted. Let's call this an action or accountability plan. Depending upon the limitation, it may be appropriate to hire someone else to fulfill the leadership obligation. Remember that great leaders understand their limitations and then surround themselves with the appropriate talent to help them accomplish what God has called them to do.

RESULTS

We are interested in sustainable results over the long-run. Therefore, make sure that you touch base regularly with your Christian coach, accountability partner, or counselor. Keeping our eyes wide open is a vital part of the process.

CHRISTIAN LEADERSHIP WORLDVIEW: PRINCIPLE #48

All Christian leaders have workplace limitations that need to be corrected. The question is, "What are you going to do about it?" It would be inadvisable to let our limitations and blind spots override and derail other aspects of workplace leadership excellence that we bring to the organization. One should stay focused on continuous leadership improvement.

49

KEEP A CLEAR CONSCIENCE

Every human has four endowments – self-awareness, conscience, independent will and creative imagination. These give us the ultimate human freedom... The power to choose, to respond, to change.

—STEPHEN COVEY

T he best way for marketplace Christian leaders to keep a clear conscience is to practice the "Golden Rule" in the workplace and make decisions that align with the principles, promises, and precepts of God's Word. People should always treat others in the way they want to be treated. Keeping a clear conscience is a prerequisite for performing the king's duties to *protect*. It's one of those nonnegotiable items on the slate of vital leadership traits. It doesn't mean that leaders will always make decisions that are easy or popular with those who follow but that leaders will make decisions and take actions that are in the best interest of the people and the organization by creating a workplace environment that is fair and equitable for all. Pleasing everyone is not a Christian leader's duty or call.

> Thou wilt keep him in perfect peace, whose mind is stayed on thee: because he trusteth in thee. (Isa. 26:3)

The easiest way to live righteously and be at peace at work is to have our heart, mind, and soul stayed on the Lord Jesus Christ while trusting in Him. I look at this verse as one who has a God-consciousness throughout the day and puts into action the sacred trust referred to above. There is a stark contrast and difference between the intellectual knowledge of God in the workplace and the effectual application of the Spirit's guiding hand. One could think about things of the Lord throughout the day but fail to abide by and walk in the Spirit. I have often found myself in this unholy conundrum. It becomes an exercise of high-mindedness without the functional real-world application of caring for and loving others. This constrains the conscience and limits Christian leadership impact in the workplace.

Let's take a look at an illustration to support this position.

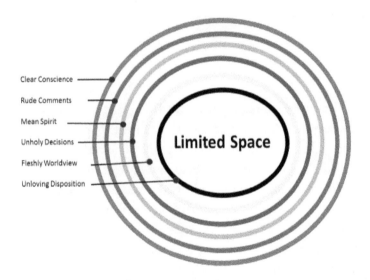

As depicted in the illustration above, Christian leaders start out with a clear conscience while operating within boundaries that are unrestrained by worldly and fleshly desires. The first circle represents a sphere in which the Holy Spirit is in full control. Workplace decisions are being made and actions are being taken that conform to Biblical standards and please the Lord. But suddenly, things take a turn for the worse when the enemy attacks and we succumb to the pressure of the world's way of thinking.

For all that is in the world, the lust of the flesh, and the lust of the eyes, and the pride of life, is not of the Father, but is of the world. (1 John 2:16)

With each successive ring and error in judgment, we confine and narrow the Holy Spirit's leading and limit our capacity to lead. In a sense, we shrink the impact that we can have at work because of our unrighteous and unholy approach to the workplace. The smaller the ring, the less influence we will be able to exert with our fellow co-workers along with our ability to impact the workplace culture.

Fortunately, Christian leaders who have erred can ask for forgiveness from the Lord and from those at work who they have negatively impacted and "turn" back to the Lord's standards of workplace leadership excellence and begin anew. Assuming the infractions have not been egregious or unlawful in nature, repentance will allow one to continue to run the race that is set before him or her in the workplace environment and make a difference for Christ.

Remember that it takes a lifetime to define and demonstrate our godly Christian character, but it only takes one poor decision to render our influence inoperable and void.

CHRISTIAN LEADERSHIP WORLDVIEW: PRINCIPLE #49

Please pray that the Lord will give you the strength and wisdom to leave an enduring and God-honoring legacy in the workplace. Desire to seek His face every morning for the sustenance needed to keep a clear conscience and make an impact for His Kingdom. The workplace is a Christian goldmine! We need to be about the business of claiming the workplace for the Savior!

Conclusion

FADING INFLUENCE OR RENEWED VIGOR

As the world moves further and further away from the godly values that have made our culture strong, Christians in the workplace should endeavor to dig in their heels and make a difference. Today, Bible-believing Christians are being forced out of leadership positions because of our religious beliefs. The algebraic math on this issue isn't very complicated.

Let's assume for a moment that Christian beliefs and values are represented as an "X" value. Christianity = X. Let's also assume that the beliefs and values being espoused by the Secular Humanists are represented as a "Y" value. Secular Humanism = Y. Across this great country, corporations are forcing Christians to support "Y" value standards of immorality and unethical behavior that directly contradict what we hold close to our heart through Bible doctrine. The human resources departments we have in America have made an "art" of moving people around in organizations to avoid religious discrimination lawsuits. Talented Christian men and women are being pigeonholed into positions of lesser impact because they are unwilling to support the ugly and perverse Secular Humanist agenda. It happens every day, and it is getting worse.

CHRISTIANITY = X

- We have a holy and righteous Creator God who rules the Universe.

- God so loved the world that He sent His only Son to die on a cross for the sins of mankind.
- Christianity has a "big tent" and has room for all who come to Christ as Savior.
- Marriage is between a man and a woman.
- Homosexuality is sin.
- God made human beings both male and female.
- Gender confusion and alteration is sin.
- Absolute truth stems from the Word of God.
- The Bible is the source of all truth.

SECULAR HUMANISM = Y

- The greatness of mankind and his thinking will rule the Universe.
- Man is innately good and, over time, humans can become better all on their own.
- Secular Humanism is open to all who share their values and beliefs that God doesn't exist.
- Marriage is whatever man says it is.
- Homosexuality is a preference that displays one's uniqueness and authenticity.
- God made people whose gender identities are what they believe themselves to be.
- Gender identity is a choice and a value or standard that should be embraced by all.
- Absolute truth is relative.
- Man lives out and experiences truth as he is further enlightened.

THE COLLISION COURSE

Can you see the collision course that has been going on for decades in the workplace? Many corporations have made sensitivity training mandatory for all their employees. If one is in a position of leadership, that person is expected to be in lock-step with Secular Humanist values. If an employee doesn't conform, one of two things will happen. First, the employee will be moved into positions where they have no one reporting to them. The employee will be given some kind of special assignment or special project within the organization and told that the assignment will benefit his or her career in the long run. However, in most cases, after the assignment ends, the employee flounders around and never finds another team to lead. This tactic is a subtle way to move those employees out of the way who don't share the organization's Secular Humanist values and beliefs.

Second, they will either let the person go or revalue the position (same job with less pay) to the point that the person cannot afford to stay.

The exciting aspect of our dilemma is that Christians do have a choice. They can either roll over and justify their support of the ungodly standards as being part of the job, or they can stand up for what they believe in and refuse to administer the enemy's agenda. Bottom line, if one jumps on board and participates with the sensitivity training, that person is helping to define a worldview that is not his or her own.

I believe that bold men and women in the workplace can bring a new sense of commitment and vigor to the fight for Christian freedom and liberty. We can reinsert ourselves back into the fight by living out our faith and not giving in. It is a call to spiritual arms for all Christians who operate in the vocational realm! As C.S. Lewis said, "There is no neutral ground in the universe: every square inch, every split second, is claimed by God and counter-claimed by Satan."[1] Dig in, and fight for what you believe in. Praise God!

---

[1] C.S. Lewis, *The Seeing Eye, And Other Selected Essays from Christian Reflections* (Random House, 1967).

ABOUT US

Christian Leadership Worldview International (clwi.org) offers high-quality leadership training and development solutions at affordable prices. Our desire is to help grow leaders around the world through one conversation at a time. We strive to impact organizations by improving employee morale, reducing turnover, increasing productivity, and fostering collaboration and teamwork as well as creating personal growth and self-improvement opportunities. In addition, CLWI takes a special interest in the development of young student leaders around the world.

Using a mission board, non-profit organizational model, CLWI has the flexibility to offer customized leadership solutions through a menu of options while being a low-cost industry provider. We are ready to serve the leadership needs of both employees and students alike. We are a Christian organization that uses Biblical principles and concepts as the foundation for organizational development and key learning experiences. Our focus is to point people to Jesus Christ, and we do it through training and development.

We believe that working through local churches is fundamental to who we are as an organization. As we help to grow Christian leaders on the one hand as well as evangelize and spread the gospel message on the other, we want to make sure that everyone is interacting with a local body of Christian believers as the Bible instructs us to do.

Our Logo

The prayer of Christian Leadership Worldview International (clwi.org) and its partners is that the logo represents a bold, compassionate, willing, and activist participant against a backdrop of global organizational need. CLWI wants our logo to signify the desperate need around the world for Christian leadership training and development in small-

to medium-sized organizations. We believe that many organizations of today are being left out of this needed spiritual growth opportunity as they focus primarily on financial, social, environmental, and technological concerns, leaving out the spiritual development of their people.

The silhouette behind the podium in the logo depicts the "call to action" for Christian leaders to stand up and get involved. While leadership does not always mean being front-and-center in a crowd, it does mean teaching, training, challenging, and motivating people to reach new heights of spiritual development. From those who lead through prayers kneeling at a bedside to those who are called to preach and teach the word in front of thousands, we must be willing to move beyond self for the benefit of others.

CPSIA information can be obtained
at www.ICGtesting.com
Printed in the USA
FFHW020424191118
49396408-53801FF